The CHURCH
of TANGO

A MEMOIR

C H E R I E
M A G N U S

MIRASOL

P R E S S
LOS ANGELES
BUENOS AIRES

All of the following events are true, but several names have
been changed..

Printed in the United States of America

https:/createspace.com/3733773
tangocherie@gmail.com

ISBN-13: 978-0615573540
ISBN-10: 0615573541

ACKNOWLEDGMENTS

*Thanks to the Buenos Aires English Writers'
Group who encouraged me when the
going got tough. I always felt they had my back.*

*Thanks to Helen Coyle who did a painstaking
professional edit that inspired the
rewrite.*

*Thanks to Robin Tara (of Tara Tango Shoes) for
all of her fabulous cover and book design work
along with her patience working with me.*

*Thanks to Katy Metz de Martinez for the back
cover photo of me she shot during
lunch at Las Violetas.*

*Thanks to the readers, who will be in my per-
sonal Hall of Fame forever: Elizabeth
Brinton, Roland Vasin, Patrice Wynne, Nancy
Ingle, Dee Schwartz.*

*Thanks to my friends in L.A. who held me up
when I was falling down.*

For Ruben,
The journey brought me to you.

Para Ruben,
El viaje me llevó a vos.

I have the soul of a suitcase,
but of a suitcase that returns...
my life, really, was always that:
a going and a returning...
Like the criminals, like the fiancées
and like the bill collectors:
I always return ...

~ E. S. Discepolo, writer of tangos

Foreword

Home is Where the Cat Is

I never think of the future. It comes soon enough.

~ Albert Einstein

It was finally obvious how to follow my bliss. And so I packed up Phoebe the Cat and moved to Buenos Aires, leaving Mexico, Los Angeles, and France above the Equator and in my heart. I felt so Argentine, what with the nostalgia for my past, the longing for my lost loved ones, and the healing joy of dancing tango in the present.

After so many international moves, my money box was empty. Now I must depend on my monthly pension. When Argentina's terrible inflation rose higher and higher, I started to panic. But one year after arriving in Buenos Aires, I met a milonguero who became my dance partner and my partner in life. When I first saw him dance, I knew he expressed the music the way I felt it in my heart. Together we competed and were finalists in the Buenos Aires Metropolitan Tango Championships of 2006. After that we became in demand for teaching classes, and so now several years later it is our joy and our job, as well as extra income. In 2011 TripAdvisor.com listed us as the #2 attraction of Buenos Aires, so the students keep on coming. What a surprise to be teaching the tango in Argentina! Perhaps twenty years ago I wished for and imagined a different future—that of growing old with Jack, grandchildren visiting in our comfortable home, family trips to our apartment in Evian-les-Bains, France.

But I guess I ended up where I was meant to be.

Into a dancer you have grown
From a seed somebody else has thrown
Go on ahead and throw some seeds of your own
And somewhere between the time you arrive and the time you go
May lie a reason you were alive but you'll never know.

~ Jackson Browne

CHAPTER 1

THE CAFÉ DE L'ESPÉRANCE

We must let go of the life we have planned,
so as to accept the one that is waiting for us.

~ Joseph Campbell

It was February, 1992, when I stood in my raincoat with my two suitcases in front of a locked courtyard gate in the 9th arrondissement. The airport taxi vanished, leaving me alone on the deserted street. The digicode I had brought from Los Angeles didn't unlock the big double doors of the eighteenth-century apartment building. What am I doing here? I wondered in a moment of panic. Am I completely crazy after a year of widowhood?

But just then a woman wearing a bright silk scarf over her dark winter coat opened the courtyard door, saying pleasantly, "Bonjour! Alors, entrez!" before setting off down the street toward the pealing bells of the church of Notre Dame de Lorette. I propped open the heavy green door with one bag, hauled the rest of my gear over the threshold, and entered the courtyard as Alice must have entered Wonderland.

I had always wondered what was behind those huge doors I saw in French films that hid Parisians' private lives from the curious tourist on the street, and now as I lugged my baggage across the court I took a good look. Large and square, completely enclosed on all four sides by the six-storied building, the courtyard's only items of interest were the gray cobblestones and a metal fountain for, I supposed, watering horses a hundred years ago. The perfume of Sunday-morning coffee floated from several windows.

Madame de Chardon waited in her open doorway as I got off the minuscule cage elevator on the third floor. Madame, small-boned and elegant, "d'un certain âge," with a pink artificial flower already pinned to her chignon, surveyed my abundant American belongings now filling up the small entry hall of her apartment. "Bienvenue, Madame Magnus. Je suis enchantée de faire votre connaissance." We shook hands firmly up and down exactly twice in the prescribed French way.

"Would you like a cup of tea?" she asked in French, opening the curtained glass parlor doors. (Five other doors led off the tiny foyer.) While she clanged pots in the kitchen, I perched on the drab flowered sofa and studied the portraits hanging from picture rails and porcelain boxes balanced on lace doilies on Directoire marble tables. Madame brought in teabag tea and packaged cookies with panache on a tarnished silver tray.

"I was able to keep my large apartment in this good quartier by renting out the two extra bedrooms to students." At this she peered over her glasses at me as if to ascertain I wasn't too old to study French. "Furthermore," Madame continued, "I enjoy meeting people from around the world— and occasionally practicing the English."

To me the apartment was very French and therefore charming, over two hundred years old with high ceilings and marble fireplaces in each room. Madame ushered me round on a guided tour, and I gaped at the exposed pipes and conduits that ran every which way, the laundry draping from clotheslines crossing the ceilings, and dusty curtains hiding caches of God-knew-what in every niche and corner. I didn't care that the two towels Madame handed me were threadbare, or that the bureau drawers were full of things belonging to people long-since departed, or that all of the fancy cornices and moldings in my room were painted a hideous bright pink. Or even that a thin layer of grime covered everything. I was in Paris.

Madame indicated that I shouldn't make myself at home in the rest of the apartment. I noticed the telephone in the dining room had a padlock on it, not that I had anyone to call. The stale cookies had left a dusty taste in my mouth, and so I went across the street to sit over a crème on the sidewalk of the Café de l'Espérance, now open and filling up with after-Mass and instead-of-Mass habitués. My ears ached with listening to them all speaking French as I stirred my coffee and looked around with amazement. Here I was, at age forty-eight, suddenly on my own in Paris, transported as if by magic. There was no place on earth I would rather be, nothing else I would rather be doing. It had been three years since I had had a moment like this. Los Angeles was far away, so was the despair and depression I had lived with for so long.

Last year Jack had been in a cancer clinic in Tijuana, the hospital of last resorts. The Mexican doctors took him off morphine so that the organic herbal treatments they prescribed would be more effective. He suffered agonies of withdrawal with sweats, hallucinations of snakes coming out of the walls, enormous pain. Even so, throughout his torment he had been uncomplaining and optimistic and brave, unlike me who had not felt the least bit courageous watching him die, just terrified.

On the first Christmas without him six weeks ago, I kept thinking about how Jack and I and the boys used to go at night to the Alameda Tracks in the belly of downtown Los Angeles to buy a glorious eight-footer at auction, fresh off the boxcars from Oregon. Winter cold down at the tracks at night, we warmed our hands over oil-drum fires. We bought our dinner from taco trucks and churro and cotton-candy wagons before piling into the pine-scented jeep to go home.

My first Christmas as a widow, I didn't feel like doing that. As soon as I would come home from work, I went straight up to bed. Adam and Jason, my sons, were still at home since the funeral, and they didn't much feel like it either. Nobody cared about celebrating Christmas or anything else. My medication for depression only caused my insides trouble and changed the taste of food, so that I completely lost my appetite too. My appetite for living had left me long ago.

I tried to make a New Year's resolution but I couldn't think of anything I wanted to do in my life, let alone in the coming year. I knew I had to sell the house and get out of my financial difficulties. I knew my grown sons had to live their own lives. I knew my mother, affected by a failing memory, couldn't help or comfort me or even understand what I was going through. I knew that each day was a mountain to climb over. I had no wishes, desires or hope, apart from freeing myself from the loneliness and pain.

Finally on New Year's Day as I lay in bed too down to get up, I realized there was something I wanted: to learn French. My love affair with France and all things French had begun with my first ballet lessons as a child. I had been thrilled to travel to France with Jack several times and to communicate, however ineptly. We had even bought and furnished an apartment with another couple in Evian-les-Bains on the shore of Lake Geneva—a last gift to me.

But I had been exploiting my three years of high school French. Maybe now was the time to do something serious about it. At my age, if I didn't become fluent pretty soon, I figured I wouldn't have a whole lot of time left to use it. Jack's too early death made me more conscious than ever of not waiting for "someday."

Linda and Steve, my Francophile neighbors next door, lent me a stack of brochures from language schools in France, and I picked one in Paris. On the second of January, I phoned my travel agent, and then I requested time off from my job at the city library. Before I left for Paris, against the advice of my doctor who was afraid I might drown myself in the Seine, I threw away the antidepressants that made food taste like rusty airplane parts. "I'm going to France and by damn I'm going to taste the food and drink!" The kids were glad that at last I wanted to do something besides cry in bed.

And now two weeks later, here I was, alone in this city of my dreams, getting ready to start school the next day. Sometimes magic can be performed with a wish and a credit card.

After my coffee, I crossed the street, and this time when I punched in the digicode, the gate opened.

***

The next morning I got up early and struggled with the "foreign" bathroom and the accompanying hot water problem, the problem being that there wasn't any. I took a cold shower, thankful that I just had my auburn mane cut short, and tried not to hose down the entire room with the hand-held shower spray as I stood in the footed tub with no shower curtain. Being tall, I was careful not to bump my head on the useless water heater suspended directly overhead. Afterwards I dabbed my lashes with mascara, something I never did in L.A.

Euphoric to have someplace in Paris that expected me, I joined the Monday-morning throng hurrying down the steps of the Place Saint-Georges Métro station. The Parisians riding the train to Concorde in elegant suits looked vastly different from the tee shirt and jogging-clad public transport commuters of L.A. I wore jeans and boots and a black leather jacket like the student I had suddenly become.

French school was the right prescription for what ailed me. No one knew me or my problems; all I had to worry about was my homework; I could be happy for a little while just being me, whoever that was. I had hope that in two weeks my French would be, if not perfect, more Parisian, more French! Suddenly I had an appetite. For the first time in years there were pleasurable things to do, learn, see, feel, taste. As I stepped on the train, I felt myself crave.

CHAPTER 2

A PASSION FOR PARIS

Everyone has two countries, his own and France.

~ Benjamin Franklin

Views of the Eiffel Tower and the glittering dome of the Invalides across the river waited for me at the top of the stairs at the Place de la Concorde. My fellow rush-hour Métro riders swept me across the rue de Rivoli and under the arcades where I searched for the French school. Block after block of boutiques displayed chunky gold jewelry and Chanel suits, Hermès silk scarves, kid gloves, Yves St Laurent leather bags, furs, Fabérgé eggs and Daum crystal, perfume, chocolate, and silk lingerie.

The artistic presentation of everything in France, from goods to food, overwhelmed me. Here, beauty was a valued virtue, an end in itself, its own commodity. And when beauty's end was to sell expensive merchandise, no detail was spared or haphazardly put together. The uncluttered windows I passed on my way to school were as exquisitely planned as paintings.

For the second time in twenty-four hours, I entered large double doors and crossed an old courtyard, this time walking up two flights of marble stairs to the French school. A couple of thin, delicate, dark-haired women musically Bonjour'd the students milling around the small waiting room. Awkward and suddenly self-conscious, I Bonjour'd in return. A clump of nervous smokers puffed away on their American cigarettes under the Non-Fumeur sign posted above them on the wall. I didn't see or hear any English, only the Germanic, Scandinavian and Japanese languages of the people taking the placement test with me.

My class had only two other students: Marcus, a twenty-five-year-old man from Munich, and Werner, a handsome young Swiss who was as smiling and ready with a joke as the German was seriously grim. Marcus was the same age as Adam, my oldest son. I was probably the oldest person in the school, faculty included. The three of us waited around a table in a small classroom for our professeur, Nathalie, who swept in like Isabelle Adjani, tossing her long dark hair off her face and smiling radiantly.

"Bonjour, tout le monde! Bien, welcome! Enchantée to meet you! How do you like Paris?" Her exotic beauty, probably North African, and her good humor made me comfortable immediately. We spent the first hour talking in French about ourselves and where we were from. Nathalie seemed fascinated by everything we said, watched us intently, and smiled with enthusiasm. For the first time ever in my French studies I used the familiar form of "tu" instead of the polite "vous" that I had learned in high school. And as illogical as I knew it was, using "tu," which I had previously been taught was reserved for family and intimates, made me feel close to these people I had just met.

At lunchtime, Werner and I crossed the street to a tabac for a salad, while tall, thin Marcus in faded jeans and a parka strode off to the Tuileries to eat the sandwich he had brought from the quartier where he was staying. Werner was about my height of five foot seven and had buzz-cut blond hair, with summer sky-blue eyes. He wore a beautifully cut jacket over a white turtleneck with elegant wool slacks and Italian shoes. Over coffee he confided he was thirty-one, had a great job, and was only here because his company was paying for everything, plus a generous per diem. He was staying with friends in a large apartment in Saint-Germain.

"I am looking on these two weeks in Paris as a winter break. If I learn some more French, great, but it is the fun I come for! And the scenery!" He winked, and our laughter blended with the rest of the boisterous sound in the packed restaurant. How long had it been since I had laughed?

After lunch, precisely at one o'clock, Professeur Olivier, a tall aristocratic-looking Parisian with laughing eyes and curly dark hair, began the afternoon class. More organized and scheduled than Nathalie, he explained to us what we would be doing the next two weeks: all the classes were intensive, French only, with grammar exercises, conversation, literature, compositions, and dialogues.

Sent by their employers, my two Germanic classmates both insisted on a business emphasis. I was disappointed in not spending more time listening to the cassette tapes of poetry and songs, and discussing art and ideas. As it was, I was so mesmerized by Professeur Olivier writing elaborate notes and diagrams with four colors of pens on the board, the subject of our lessons began not to matter.

Classes met from nine to four-thirty, and afterwards I experienced as much of Paris as I could before the shops and museums closed and night fell. Dusk was my favorite time, when the boutiques and cafés lit up one by one and made the city look even more like the "Disneyland for adults" I wrote about on the Opéra Garnier postcards I sent back home to my sons.

Paris was an amusement park to me; I was a kid in a candy store. History, beauty, art and music were everywhere. A string quartet played Vivaldi in a tiny park in front of the Sorbonne one evening when I climbed up the Métro steps on my way to a student concert. A large Peruvian band serenaded commuters in the Opéra station each night at rush hour. Lone saxophones and violin players seemed to be around each corner, often with a portable tape deck providing accompaniment. Music echoed through the tunnels of the city's underground. I heard Dave Brubeck's "Take Five" played so many different ways on so many different instruments it pretended to be the Parisian anthem.

The surprising street music is what lots of Americans like about Paris, along with the tiny bistros with lace-curtained, rain-steamed windows, discrete and elegant neon signs and old covered passages where you can take tea and dream at a sidewalk café on a rainy day. I loved winter in Paris because that was when I was there.

I went everywhere alone, yet I was never lonely. People socialized and mingled in the cafés, parks, squares in all weather. What a novelty to be jostled with polite apologies for the smallest elbow nudge, Pardon! Pardon! The animated sidewalks were such a pleasure after L.A.'s endless empty concrete ribbons that made my eyes ache in the California sun.

I heard my name everywhere. "Cherie" in French means "dear one," it's not a given name at all. I noticed that when I was introduced to a French man, he had a hard time calling me by the name reserved for his wife. On the streets, in shops, and in the park, I heard my name: mothers calling their children. And I loved it.

One didn't necessarily eat alone in Paris, even if one were alone. Near the school was Rubis, a popular and busy bistro where people shared tables. At a round wooden table with five other people on their lunch hour, a party broke out. Jokes were told, people laughed and so did I, even if I didn't entirely understand; toasts were proposed. The young woman on my left offered me a taste of her crème brulée and the man on my right bought me a glass of Cahors.

Instead of being tired from the wine, I whirled back to class through the lunchtime crowds that filled the rainy rue Saint-Honoré, exhilarated. Parisian women didn't seem to care if their fashionable shoes and beautiful legs got wet as they click-clicked past me in their high heels and mini-skirts, trailing exquisite perfume. In Los Angeles life came to a halt on the few days each year it rained, yet here the stormy weather didn't dampen the city's energy and enthusiasm, which rubbed off on me. Maybe it was the strong dark roast coffee I'd just had at Rubis, but I felt vibrant and enthusiastic, too. I wanted to dance like Gene Kelly across the wet cobblestones. Unfamiliar happiness bubbled up like a fountain of French champagne. In Paris, men flirted with me and really looked at me, and I realized for the first time in years that I was still a woman men found attractive. I had forgotten that, too.

Before I left L.A. a friend had given me the telephone number of his daughter Elizabeth, who lived in Paris with her French husband Jean-Luc and their two children, along with instructions to call and say hello. When I did, Elizabeth invited me to their apartment near the Place d'Italie.

On my way to Elizabeth's the next night, in the Tuileries Gardens I saw a carrousel spinning, glowing, dazzlingly vibrant and incongruous in the center of the gray garden. It was almost as if the voice of God were speaking from an old Cecil B. DeMille movie, only instead of light streaming down from heaven above, it came up from within the merry-go-round, saying to me: Rejoice! L'Chaim!

It was so cold it started to snow. Umbrellas sprouted up along the rue de Rivoli like so many black poppies, imitating a scene from a Caillebotte painting.

When I managed the digicode to Elizabeth and Jean-Luc's apartment in the modern high-rise, I made my way up and found the small living room was full of people and smoke.

"But you are so young!" were Elizabeth's first words as she opened the door. "You don't look like a widow! We were expecting an old lady in black! Entre, Entre! Installe-toi!"

Elizabeth herself no longer looked like a California girl, on the contrary she had le look très parisien with her tiny yet curvy figure and glossy black hair. And from what I could tell, her French was perfect. I expected it to seem odd to speak to another American in French, yet it felt perfectly natural to chatter away with Elizabeth in the language of the evening.

She and Jean-Luc introduced me around the room as "La Californienne!" Their French guests were curious: "You are here, from la Californie, alone in winter, mais pourquoi?" They were intrigued by my determination to learn their language, by how much I liked their country, and, I suppose, by my naiveté.

Bernard, a realtor who lived in the apartment next door, hovered over me, bringing me drinks, introducing me to his friends, enchanting me. He was tall for a Frenchman, and slim, with long hair and nicotine-stained fingers, in jeans and a black silk shirt under a burgundy wool blazer.

The dining table was covered with bottles of wine and whiskey, and the buffet with platters of pâté, salads, and a roast chicken. American rock and roll came from the radio. I hated to leave but the composition for Olivier's class was on my mind. Finally I said, "I must go do my homework, excusez-moi, s'il vous plait."

"Oh you Americans!" Bernard laughed. "Always thinking about tomorrow and work. We French are unconcerned about getting a good night's sleep for work the next day. How can we sleep at ten if we have not finished dinner?"

Bernard found me a taxi in the frosty night air and invited me to dinner the next night before kissing me on each cheek. "Until tomorrow," he said to me, "La Place Saint-

Georges" to the driver. I waved to him from the window as the cab took off, watching him light a cigarette in the rain.

Dinner with Bernard the next night was another party, a room full of couscous, Moroccan music, and smoke from the marijuana he grew on his balcony. At midnight I bellydanced on the coffee table with a shawl tied around my hips, certain I was dreaming. Bernard was attractive, and I was excited by his attention. I felt proud of myself that I could make new friends all in French.

Every day in class I felt myself more attracted to Olivier, his voice, his wit, his intelligence, his eyes the color of dark brown velvet, his full sensuous lips, and when he turned to write on the board, I couldn't avoid admiring his beautiful derrière covered with rough European tweed. I fantasized he was a writer, and one day in fact he admitted in class that he had published a book of poetry the previous year. I knew he must be of rather moderate means as a teacher, wearing what appeared to be old and elegantly shabby clothing. He probably lived in a tiny studio right out of Puccini's La Bohème.

All of these clues and suppositions, that he was a Byronic poet living in a Parisian garret, made him all the more romantic to me. When he gave writing assignments, I wrote my compositions as if I were writing to him, telling him about my life, and myself and then felt betrayed when, after class, I saw him throw them in the trash.

He lectured with great passion, waving his arms to punctuate and emphasize. His voice was the sexiest sound I had ever heard; his exuberance as he talked about French politics, literature and ideas, excited me. When he recommended a book by Marguerite Duras, I ran to Galignani on the rue de Rivoli at lunchtime to buy it and show it to him like a child. I stared at him in class, hypnotized. I couldn't believe that I found another man attractive. I still was so in love with Jack, missed him as if he had taken my soul with him to heaven. But there it was: I could imagine falling in love again. And it was a revelation.

One night I hid in a phone booth on the sidewalk, pretending to make calls for the benefit of the line of people waiting to use the telephone. Shivering both from the cold and from nerves, I watched for Olivier to leave the school. When I saw him come out the door under the dusk of evening with his backpack, I ran down the street after him as the shop lights began to turn on.

"Olivier! Do you want to have a drink?" Breathless from my sprint, I was aghast at my newfound boldness. He was walking in another world, and at first didn't hear me.

He looked at me in utter disbelief. "Where, when? Maintenant?"

"Now, yes! I'm going to the Opéra Garnier for the ballet, so I only have a little while. Do you want to have a drink?"

With comprehension, pleasure flooded his face, and we walked together to La Coupe D'Or on the corner. It felt so natural to take his arm, to touch him through the sleeve of his old brown leather jacket. Walking arm in arm with a man I cared about was as familiar and comfortable as breathing.

We sat at a tiny table for two hours in the café, so packed with the after work crowd that our legs had to touch. He ordered a beer, which surprised me. I thought that French people only drank wine. We talked (or rather he talked and I listened as I did in class) about life, literature, art, film, politics—the usual French café topics.

"So you attend the ballet tonight?" he asked.

"Oh yes, I was so pleased to get a ticket yesterday. D'aprés moi, le ballet est l'expréssion parfait de l'art! Using the body to express beautiful music—well, it's perfect, is all. I used to be a dancer myself," I added quietly.

"Alors, in Paris it is simple to attend the theatre. Art is everywhere." Olivier gestured grandly, the sweep of his arm taking in the crowded café.

"It's true! If you want to see a Picasso, you run out your door and twenty minutes later you're standing in front of Still Life with Caned Chair in the Hotel Salé like I did the other afternoon. How lucky you are to live here!"

"Yes, for us Parisians, art is part of our daily life." His handsome face beamed proudly at me. His manner implied that France and all things French were superior, and I couldn't have agreed more.

In our daily lunchtime discussions, Werner had bet that Olivier was single, and I had agreed, or at least I hoped he was. Nevertheless for all of my mooning over him, Olivier hadn't been flirtatious in response. He seemed like an absent-minded professor in an ivory tower, and that just made me work harder for him to notice me. Now I collected the courage to ask him a delicate question. "Do you have any children, Olivier?" I wanted to ease backward into the fact of his being married or not.

"Mais non, a cat is enough!" he laughed.

"Are you married, though? Do you have a wife?" I asked, averting my eyes, afraid to look at him, afraid of his response. I already knew that such personal questions were considered rude so soon after meeting someone in France, but

I hoped my ignorant American self could get away with it.

"Oui, j'ai une femme." He sighed, then chuckled to himself. "I have been married for twenty years."

C'est magnifique, I was crazy about a man for the first time since I fell in love with my husband so long ago, and he was married. Well, what did I expect?

"But she is never in Paris," he continued. "She is an academic and has fallen in love with Nepal. And I with my solitude," he laughed again.

When we stood up to leave, he bent down and kissed me, not the bises on the cheek, but on the lips, stunning me. The first romantic kiss I'd had in so many years. I felt like Snow White or the Sleeping Beauty. His lips were so soft, I melted into them. That kiss was all I could think about as I rushed, with no time to change into the silk blouse I had carried all day in my book bag, to the Place de l'Opéra where the illuminated Palais Garnier sat like a nineteenth-century wedding cake. That astonishing kiss was all I could think about in my sixth-row center seat as the Paris Opera Ballet danced "Cendrillon."

At the entr'acte, with a glass of champagne in my hand, I stood on the balcony overlooking the Place de l'Opéra and watched the sun set on the black slate rooftops of the Palais du Louvre. I wondered if Olivier liked ballet and if he came here with his wife.

After the performance I let myself be swept along in the crowd that flowed across the street to the Café de la Paix. Walking in alone and asking for a table for one, I felt regal, elegant, without parallel. Unlike in America, women dining alone in fine restaurants in France were flattered, fussed over and made to feel totally welcome. No woman in Paris tonight, or anywhere else in the world, could be happier than I was at that moment. It was after midnight, yet I was surrounded by laughter and animated conversation, the tinkling of china and crystal, energy.

Afterwards I hailed a taxi, and as I climbed in the radio was playing Edith Piaf. I'm living in a movie, I thought on the way back to Madame's. An Américaine in Paris!

That night I lay wide-eyed and quiet in my bed fantasizing about Olivier's kiss and his soft lips. More than anything I wanted to run my tongue over them, and I thought of myself doing that until it was time to get up for my last day in Paris. Why did he kiss me like that? What, if anything, did it mean?

To commemorate the final day of French school, my fellow students bought my lunch at a bistro on the rue Saint-Roch, a few doors from the church that still had Napoleon's bullets embedded in its walls. The three of us shared a bottle of wine. Since lunch time at the school was only an hour, it meant eating too much and drinking too quickly at a good Paris bistro, and we were a few minutes late back to Olivier's class. I felt giddy from the wine downed "like whiskey in an American western," as Werner observed with a laugh. Werner and I had lunched together almost every day and he teased me constantly, especially as now he knew I had a crush on Olivier.

I had felt like a queen in the tiny classroom, surrounded as I was by three men. Unfortunately I had often felt dense, too, as the French of the two Europeans was much more advanced than mine. Now on the last day, high from the wine, I sat at the square classroom table next to Olivier, who I could hardly look at without remembering his lips and getting a rush, and wondered about last night's kiss and if he looked at me and remembered, too. When Werner cracked a joke under his breath, I got the giggles like a teenager and had to leave the room and pace the hall, trying to recover my composure. What was happening to me? With all this adolescent behavior and heightened feelings during these past two weeks, I couldn't recognize myself anymore. Surely I was too old to act like this.

At the end of the class, after an exchange of addresses and cheek-kissing (my American exuberance won out over German reticence), I lingered while Olivier packed up his bag and then tagged along after him down the rue Saint-Honoré. Knowing he was married subdued me even though he didn't truly seem married: unlike most French husbands, he didn't wear a wedding ring, and he had a lonely, self-contained air about him. Was I just rationalizing, like so many other women infatuated with married men?

He was going to the Quartier Latin, and as we crossed the courtyard of the Louvre and the front of the glowing Pei pyramid, an icy winter wind blew the hair off our faces and the ends of our neck scarves danced behind us. We entered a gray stone alcove empty but for a mime dressed in brilliant gold; the last rays of the sun gleamed through the stone arches and illuminated him as he performed for only Olivier and me, mimicking lovers, during the few seconds it took us to cross the arcade and head out towards the Seine and the Pont des Arts.

"I can't follow you all over Paris. Let's say au revoir here." I stopped in front of a cheerfully busy brasserie, and looked up at him expectantly.

"Tu veux boire quelque chose?"He glanced at his watch as he asked me as I hoped he would, to have a drink with him.

We sat close together once again at a tiny table facing the street, sheltered from the cold by big plate glass windows. "When will you be coming back to Paris?" he asked with what I hoped was personal interest.

I was surprised to hear myself reply, "As soon as I can. Perhaps en automne." These past two weeks had given my life back to me, and now, addicted, I suddenly realized I wanted more. "I am going by train to Evian-les-Bains tomorrow morning to spend a week. My late husband and I bought an apartment on the south shore of Lake Geneva with another couple, friends from Los Angeles. If you would ever like to go there for a weekend or a week or two, with your wife, of course, I would be glad to lend it to you." Olivier looked at me in surprise. "Sincerely. It just sits there empty most of the time."

The truth was that I wanted him to sleep in my bed, even with his wife. I wanted to imagine him naked under my feather quilt.

"Perhaps we shall. Thank you," he touched my arm. "Bon retour, alors, come back soon to Paris. I am sorry, now I must leave to keep my appointment. I have enjoyed meeting you and having you in my class."

This time I was prepared for his kiss and didn't move

or breathe for the tiny time we touched until he took his lips from mine. I sat in the crowded café for a long time after he left, just smiling to myself.

CHAPTER 3

THE FRENCH CONNECTION

There is a time to mourn ...and a time to dance!

~ Ecclesiastes 3-4

The bullet-nosed TGV—the high-speed train of Très Grande Vitesse—blasted out of the Gare de Lyon towards the southeast. Watching the winter countryside speed past at 180 mph, I wondered what would I do in the little country town besides visit the cemetery. It had been four months since Jack's ashes were buried amid a conflagration of chrysanthemums in the village of Lugrin where our apartment was, and I was afraid of falling apart away from the distractions of Paris. My lips were still warm from Olivier's goodbye kiss. Now I had to come face to face with my loneliness again.

The TGV entered a long tunnel, and when it emerged we were in the Alps, all frosted with snow. The train sped along next to the Rhône river and soon I could see Lake Geneva, or Lac Léman to the French, from my window. At the end of the line was Evian-les-Bains and the village of Lugrin, 6 km to the east, my destination.

I dragged my luggage across the station's tracks, under the cast iron and glass Belle Époque roof, through the freezing empty depot, and out to the taxi stand. Tightening my coat against the bitter wind, I climbed into a cab and off we went past the resort town of Evian-les-Bains and on to Lugrin. The French Alps rose on the right, and Switzerland shone in the sun on the other side of the lake on the left. It was a clear, cold, bare tree afternoon in February, the world seemed old and solid. I felt at peace.

While rolling up the shutters on the apartment's many windows, turning on the hot water heaters and the heat, I heard a familiar thump! thump! from the kitchen. Edith was on her balcony next door, banging my window with the end of a broomstick. I threw the window open. "Le téléfone arab," she pointed to the broom.

"Edith! Je suis contente de te voir!" We grinned at each other.

"Viens! viens!" she gestured impatiently, and leaving my unpacking and inspection of the apartment, I ran down the six flights of stairs of my building, and up the six flights of hers, exploding into the Berengers' apartment. Edith's husband Michel, their daughter Floriane, son Fabrice, and Michel's mother, who I called Mémé along with the rest of the family, were all gathered around the glorious view of Lac Léman with champagne flutes in their hands, watching the sunset. A savory bouquet from their open kitchen scented the room, and their table was set for six. It was really true, I was home.

Michel and Edith insisted I have lunch and dinner with them every day during my week's stay in Lugrin. At first I protested, and then I just started showing up at meal times. To heck with formalities and pretense, I gave in to being cared for, and it felt wonderful. Edith's cooking was as good as any

Michelin restaurant, and no one spoke a word of English, excellent practice for my French.

Edith and Michel were my age, and their two children, Fabrice and Floriane, were in their twenties. Jack and I had met them when we bought the apartment three years before. Floriane, on her first trip away from home, had come to stay with Jack and me for six months last year. It had been right before Jack died, and a bond was forged between our two families. Jack had told Floriane she was like the daughter he never had. Maybe the beautiful Floriane hadn't learned much English, but we had learned to love and care for one another.

Later, over martinis at the Kiwi Bar in the neighboring village of Thonon, I confessed to Floriane."J'ai le béguin pour mon professeur à Paris, tu sais. He's married, but he kissed me, not on the cheek, but on the lips!"

"Les lèvres?" said Floriane, shocked.

"Is that a French custom? I didn't know what to think, but I liked it."

"Mais non!" she said, and we both giggled.

I could never have shared my crush on Olivier with conservative, traditional Edith. Born and raised in the small village, she was a country girl who nevertheless was curious about life elsewhere, one reason she sent her teenaged daughter to Los Angeles to visit us and to experience a bigger more cosmopolitan world. Even a trip to Lyon was rare for them, let alone Paris.

I did mention to Edith that my French teacher had played tapes of chansons in class and I was enchanted. She then took me shopping in the next town along the lake for some Yves Montand cassettes, as well as an album of a dead Belgian singer I had never heard of—Jacques Brel singing his own songs. "You must know Brel, Cherie!" Edith, small boned and slim with a gamin haircut, never missed a chance to show her pride in being French.

Listening to this music was an epiphany. The energy and passion in their voices, the beauty of the French language, the emotion and poetry of Brel's songs. Feelings, emotions, urges and surges, I wasn't sure which ones, raged in me. I found my way back to the Woolworth's-like Prisunic in Thonon on my own and bought all of the Montand and Brel cassettes they had, as well as some Charles Trenet, Georges Brassens, and Gilbert Bécaud, all filed under the Musique Francaise section.

The hot-blooded French music aroused me so, filled me with such long-dormant longings and joy, that one night, listening, by only the light of the log fire high above the lake, I got up and danced naked in front of the dark windows with the lights of Lausanne twinkling far away across the black water. I'm alive! And I'm in love with Montand, with the long-dead Brel, with all the men, and women in France!

For my last night in France, Edith and I made plans to go to the spectacle at the Belle Époque-period Evian Casino. Edith was always ready for a bit of fun and loved to make special occasions out of everything. Living in a country village made her eager for something different, for a bit of excitement. For me, this was a special event; the past three weeks had taught me a whole lot more than French. Probably I would miss Jack every day of my life, but I learned I still was able to enjoy myself and maybe I could love again one day. This was a completely new idea to me after wanting to bury myself along with Jack. I couldn't have imagined finding another man attractive, or that I would ever feel joy again. But now after Paris, I saw it might be possible.

I wore black wool pants with a stretchy black top and Edith dressed like the elegant Frenchwoman she was in a navy suit, white blouse, and a red, white and navy silk scarf. The apartment building's femme de ménage was at the Berengers' during the apéritif hour, and when she heard about the nightclub plans, her face lit up. And so Edith invited the cleaning lady, too. The petite Madame Blanc went home to change, and came back after dinner in rhinestone harlequin glasses and chandelier earrings that brushed the shoulders of her fuzzy white angora sweater appliquéd with feathers and sequins. She wore leggings and high-heeled black boots and carried a plastic bag with low-heeled shoes because, as she explained, the boots weren't comfortable for dancing.

After the Les Dollies Dollies show, a mini-Folies Bergère, a mirrored ball descended from the ceiling, and a DJ booth rolled from the wings. Since there were few people in the nightclub, I didn't think anyone would dance, but a woman in beige began to dance alone to the American disco music. She danced not to show off herself, her clothes or her dancing ability, but for her own enjoyment; unselfconsciously she moved to the music in a restrained and delicate way, occasionally closing her eyes No one was paying any attention to the woman dancing in her own world. But I watched her. Was she dancing alone because she had no partner, didn't need one, or didn't want one? I had never seen solo social dancing before; in Los Angeles everyone had to have a partner as a ticket onto the dance floor. Might I dance alone too?

A man left the bar and his drink and approached the dance floor. I thought, uh oh, he's going to try to pick up the dancing woman. But he took his place on the dance floor and also began to dance a solo, unmindful of the beige lady.

Madame Blanc leaned over to me and asked, "Vous voulez danser?" She had exchanged her boots for what looked like house slippers.

"Oui, je suppose, but with who?"

"Avec moi!" the cleaning lady said.

"'Allez-y, Cherie!" Edith encouraged.

Madame Blanc and I took the floor. Without her high-heeled boots she was about a foot shorter than I was, and we probably made a strange couple indeed. At first I felt awkward. I hadn't danced since before Jack became ill, more than three years ago. Soon though I got into it, and flailed away in complete abandon, letting the pulsing beat move me. Madame Blanc seemed surprised at the sudden exuberance of her partner, but she too made the most of her time on the dance floor.

The only other people out there with us, besides the two soloists, were an old couple locked in an embrace too powerful for the disco music to separate. They tangoed erotically around the floor as the stout lady's slip slipped lower below her print dress and her bra strap fell down her pudgy naked arm. Her partner's gray toupee slid a bit more forward with each tango dip. They were oblivious to all but each other. I envied them.

As we rejoined Edith at the small round cocktail table and sank into the red plush easy chairs, breathing heavily, a man approached from the bar and invited me to dance. I felt paralyzed not knowing what the protocol was in France. The others encouraged me, and soon I was out on the floor once again, this time doing the American swing with all my might. We never got to talk or exchange names or countries, but I felt like Ginger to his Fred, connected by the silent international language of dance, a language I really understood.

At two in the morning, it was time for me to leave as I had to get an early start the next morning for my flight back to L.A. Exiting the nightclub through the casino, I impulsively dropped a ten-franc coin into a slot machine and was not a bit surprised that three cherries came up. I scooped my winnings out of the tray and divided them up between us, Madame Blanc putting her coins into the top of one of the black boots which had suddenly reappeared on her feet.

Laughing, the three of us linked arms, as French women do on the street to indicate they're not looking for company and are complete among themselves, and went out into the cold black night, the mist from the lake surrounding us like a secret.

───

Rain pounded the roof as the alarm rang just a couple of hours later in my bedroom overlooking the lake. In a short time I would be back home in Los Angeles and back to work at the library. I hoped I could hang on to my newfound vitality in the middle of the old grind. I hoped, too, that one day I might see Olivier again.

When I arrived in Lugrin from Paris last week, I had thrown out the withered chrysanthemums left from the festival of Toussaint in November, and planted some heather that would bloom all winter on Jack's grave. Now, rushing in the dark wet morning to get to the Geneva airport, I stopped my loaded rental car from Evian in front of the cemetery gates and ran up the shallow incline to Jack's tomb to leave the red rose I had bought the day before. Jack, you don't have to worry about me any more, I'm going to be all right. I want to live, and I know now that I want to live in France. I just have to figure out how.

> *Mon coeur ouvrait les bras...*
> *Je volais je le jure*
> *Je jure que je volais...*

> ~ Jacques Brel

CHAPTER 4

THE BODY AND SOUL WALTZ

He turns our mourning into dancing!

~ Psalms 30:11

Joie de vivre carried me back to Los Angeles; I barely needed TWA. Paris, the divine City of Light, which can take lives down into the depths of its unfathomable river Seine, had given my life back to me.

My boys were happy to see me back home with hope and plans for the future after mourning so long. Their lives were still disorganized and off-track as far as I could see, but they were adults and had the right to choose their own mistakes. I didn't tell them what to do, nor did they tell me. We all knew we loved each other and were trying to do the best we could under the circumstances. I was upset that both of them seemed to be turning their backs on the artistic careers they had spent their teenaged years successfully developing. Neither Adam nor Jason wanted my advice or help, and didn't ask for any. I wished I could send them along the paths that I thought would make them happy, but it wasn't up to me. They didn't offer input to my life apart from Adam's, "Follow your bliss, mom." And I tried to be quiet and let them follow theirs. They seemed glad that I wanted something—even to live in a foreign country—after so long of not wanting to live at all.

"Escargot A Gogo," was among my wilder schemes for a way to earn my living in France, an import-export business that was also ecologically positive. Southern California is overrun by the descendants of the French snails that had escaped the personal escargot farm of a French immigrant gourmet in the nineteenth century. I imagined contracting with homeowners, gardeners and nurseries to gather them up on a regular basis. For a fee, of course. This was infinitely preferable (and more politically correct) to poisonous snail bait or even the custom of putting out shallow pie pans of beer, which, theory has it, lures the snails to drink—they get drunk, fall horns first into the beer pan and drown. I would harvest sober snails, pack them in boxes of lettuce to let them clean themselves naturally, and fly them to France where they would be eaten. For another fee. You could spend March to October in country gardens in France and never see a snail because they had all been eaten. Now they are just grown on snail farms. The huge and healthy, fat and juicy California escargot would be a gourmet luxury item in a country where no price is ever too high for good food.

I could work in a French library—they used our familiar Dewey Decimal System—or as a waitress in a Parisian café. I had waited tables when I was at UCLA and enjoyed it. Imagine doing it in Paris! I would meet the customers and improve my French. It came naturally for me to serve people, to give them what they wanted. Not just a librarian in a public library, hadn't I been a wife and mother?

Now back in L.A. I went to work at the library with renewed enthusiasm, knowing there was a different future in store for me than working at the same job until retirement, living alone till I died in the same city where I was born. I used to love being a librarian, as I used to enjoy so many things before Jack's illness. Once I naively said that my job was so much fun I would be happy to do it as a volunteer. It was no longer such a pleasure when I had to toil to earn enough money to live and, above all, for the health insurance that was so all-important in the States.

The conditions at the branch library where I worked had also changed. The historic brick building with stained glass windows nestled in a tiny park that I had been enchanted to work in was now closed for earthquake fortification in case of the Big One. The books and staff had moved five blocks away into rental space in a cheaply built office building on Wilshire Boulevard. The children's librarian was on maternity leave and the branch manager left to take care of family business. That left me, the young adult librarian, as acting manager and chief bottle-washer. Doing the work of three jobs was not as bad as missing the old camaraderie of my two professional co-workers. I felt lonely in the private office of the Senior Librarian, arbitrating staff disputes and writing reports. What I still found tremendously satisfying, and even exciting was being the liaison between answers and questions, books and readers, information and searchers. Every patron was unique, each meeting with the public surprising in its own way.

There were also French classes to take, French movies to see, French culture and history to read, letters to write to new French friends, all in preparation for the time when I could move to France. I no longer thought about ending my life. I gave Jack's medications—little purple morphine pills and blue pills for sleeping and white codeine pills for more pain—that I had been hoarding in my depression "just in case" to my therapist, who said it was the best present she ever received.

Jack had never gotten depressed, even when he was sick. Always with an even disposition, he amazed me. When he was learning self-hypnosis for pain control, I was there in the office of the psychologist, who put him under and had him imagine being at the end of a long hallway with many closed doors. Jack had to pick a door and open it. The doctor asked, "What do you see inside the room, Jack?" And Jack replied in his calm way from his trance, "Nothing. The room is empty." When I undertook to learn self-hypnosis myself to help me deal with the huge issues in front of me, the therapist had me face the same long hall and pick a door. Opening a door in my mind, I found unspeakable horrors, terrifying nightmares, and terrors of the worst order and, slamming it, I came out of the trance screaming. Jack was the only person I ever knew who wasn't neurotic, probably the only person with a secret room in his mind full only of light and air.

"I never had so much sex in my life as I had in France," I confided to my friend Donna over dinner at a Westwood bistro a week after my return.

"With who?" Donna asked, surprised, her faint blond eyebrows lifting so high they almost disappeared into her curly hair.

"With myself!" I answered, and we both doubled over in hysterics. We giggled and guffawed until our stomachs hurt. It felt so good to laugh like that, the first time in so many years. Donna, a fellow librarian, was a new widow too, and had also recently begun to be attracted to other men. I told her about my fascination with Olivier and she understood. We had started to hope again.

We were on our way to a grief workshop at UCLA and we tried to pull ourselves together in the hallway and to adopt suitable somber expressions before going in to join the circle of grievers, people who had paid perfectly good money to cry.

It was my long and happily married friend Nancy who encouraged me over lunch a few days later to write to Olivier. Nancy had stuck by in thick and thin, and was the only one of my friends to drive down to Tijuana to visit Jack in the hospital. She was a real salt of the earth kind of person, and now she was advising me to "Tell him he's a fascinating man who you would like to get to know better and see if he answers, Why not? You can add him to your list of friends in France. At the very least maybe you can be pen pals and practice writing in French." She shrugged and smiled. She had hung in there with me during the two years of Jack's dying, and was always ready to drop everything for a cup of tea and a chat in her cozy kitchen.

Writing the letter to Olivier energized me. The morning I dropped it in the mail box, I played the French songs on my car's tape deck even louder, so involved in singing along and feeling the music, it was a miracle I didn't have an accident as I bounced in my seat in time to George Brassens down Sunset Boulevard.

I felt compelled to half skip down the sidewalk. I wanted to spin in circles at the top of the white library steps in the April sun with the blue sky framed by red hibiscus blossoms, turning, pivoting to the Jacques Brel song I heard in my head.

> *J'aimais courir jusqu'à tomber*
> *J'aimais la nuit jusqu'au matin*
> *Je n'aimais rien non j'ai adoré*
> *Tu vois je vous aimais déjà*

> ~ Jacques Brel

In bed that night I couldn't sleep for thoughts of Olivier receiving, then reading, my letter in its pink envelope. What would he think? Would he remember me for a few minutes before throwing it away?

I calculated how long it would take for Olivier to receive the letter, how long he might take to answer, how long before I could hear from him. I added a few extra days for good measure. I looked forward to coming home every night to the mail, sometimes even calling home asking one of my sons to check the mailbox. When there was nothing after three months, I gave up, thinking, well at least I tried (my future epitaph, I decided.)

Then one day Adam called me at the library. "Mom, you got a letter from France." Olivier had answered, aloofly, dryly, reservedly, not really saying much, but he had answered. I propped the envelope against the coffee mug that held my pens on my desk where I could see it and remember that there was, indeed, hope.

Until my trip to Paris, hope had been missing from

my life ever since the moment of Jack's diagnosis three years ago. When the doctor called me in from the waiting room and shut the office door, I sat down next to Jack and gripped his hand with both of mine. "I'm sorry," said Dr Carson, "there is nothing I can do."

The life we knew for so many happy years suddenly ceased to exist. Passion and lust—for life, for art and music, for people, for each other—ended that day in the doctor's office. The doctor's words destroyed our future and made the present unbearable. On automatic pilot we shook hands politely with Dr Carson and thanked him before going out into the world of cancer, abandoned on a strange planet. With all the worrying I had done all my life, I never dreamed of something as bad as this.

How could Jack be so sick? He was the picture of health, athletic and fit, handsome and vital. He had lived all his life in moderation and never smoked, nor was he overweight. Such a good man, doing legal pro bono work for the poor, on the Church Council, giving time, energy, money, and expertise to whoever needed it. Such a kind and gentle man, one who deserved only the best life had to offer. And this man had an early death sentence? My faith wasn't challenged. I knew God's ways weren't our ways. I knew bad things happened to good people. It wasn't why us, but, it had to be somebody, why not us? Why not Jack? But oh it hurt. He continued to go to work, to play golf and tennis, to have lunch with friends, and to make plans for the future. He was going to fight, and by God, I would help him as much as I could.

I struggled to ignore my own fear and loss, but I wasn't

as positive as he was. Having always bared our souls to each other, now I put on a front for the first time in our lives together. Inside I was in mourning for our future, all our plans for retirement, for grandchildren. When we went to see "The Phantom of the Opera," the romantic plot, the Paris Opera setting, the overblown passion of the music, the emotions unleashed kept me awake for weeks. For the first time I couldn't share my feelings with Jack, my partner, the love of my life, the person who really knew me and still loved me with all his heart. How could he comfort me?

Music now stirred up too many emotions that I couldn't handle and didn't want to remember. I never played my tapes or even the car radio anymore. I still played the piano for hours trying to release the pain through my fingers, usually with a vodka and orange juice on the music stand. It was only in the shower and in the car with the windows rolled up tight that I cried, setting free my rage and grief. I screamed until my throat hurt, driving to work at the library and back again. Soon my tears flowed automatically whenever I turned on the shower or started the engine of my car. I didn't want to remember the passion that had been so important in our life together and was now gone forever after Jack's cancer surgery, a horrifying, unbelievable orchiectomy, or surgical castration, in order to cut the supply of testosterone which fed the cancer. I only wanted strength to get through each day, the power to comfort and care for Jack without showing him my despair.

I knew then that there would be no more romance in my marriage, no more hope. I would never make love again in my life.

CHAPTER 5

COWBOY CHA CHA

Our lives are better left to chance.
I could have missed the pain,
but I'da had to miss the dance.

~ Garth Brooks

I was back in L.A. and back to work but not in the old grind. My life, my future now opened up before me, even at my age and in my circumstances. I was ready to try new things and to meet new people. My sons had their own survival problems and weren't concerned with mine. But I was able to convince Jason to check out the new trendy talk of the town dance club with me. Previously a coffee shop, now Rhinestones 'n' Rawhide was the place to be. I couldn't imagine yuppie Los Angeles westsiders so excited about a country and western club. I wanted to see it for myself.

Married young and for so long, I had never gone to a bar or a club alone. Now curious and timid and wanting to dance again, I convinced Jason to check it out with me on a Friday night. We played K-FROG, the country radio station, on the drive over to get into the cowboy mood, but the twangy music was not enough preparation for the time-and-place warp we found inside the open doors of Rhinestones 'n' Rawhide. First of all, everybody in the club was white! I had never seen a large gathering in a public place in L.A. without black and brown faces.

Half the men sported cowboy hats and quite a few of the women did too. Women wore tiny denim shorts with ruffles, short twirly skirts, or little print dresses with cowboy boots. One beautiful girl wore full leather chaps over her tight Levi's, accentuating her perfectly round rear. Plaid shirts and jeans seemed to be the dominant attire for the men. There was not a square-dance dress in sight and I suddenly felt all wrong in baggy jeans and a plaid blouse. The dress code was sexy Hollywood cowboy.

The dancing couples moved counter-clockwise in the Texas Two-Step, slow-slow, quick-quick, slow-slow-quick-quick, around the elevated dance floor. Groups of people stood talking near the floor, around the pool tables, and jammed in front of the three bars.

"Jason, the girls here are pretty cute, aren't they?"

"Damn straight!" he said with a fake country drawl. "They's a lot of good lookin' eye candy heah!"

I didn't know what to think about all these cowboys. "The men look a little strange though, don't they?"

"Dey look like dey is inbred, sho' nuf. Hey, Ma, which 'un of des dudes ya like?"

"Well, I guess that tall guy over at the bar isn't too bad," wanting to play along.

Jason moseyed over to the dude in question, me in his wake. "Evenin'. How ya' all?" He carried on like this, intending to get this fellow to dance with me, until I caught Jason's eye, and shook my head, laughing.

"Come on, Jason. Let's you and me do this "Electric Slide' or 'Glide' or whatever."

We joined the people forming tight lines on the dance floor. We faked our way through that one and also the Cowboy Cha Cha, but the "Horseshoe" proved impossible—one of those rare asymmetrical dances in which each step was different, combining three's and one's and two's. It was a couple's dance done in the sweetheart position, side by side, to a haunting country song. The dance charmed me and I made up my mind to learn it at the free dance lessons the club gave every night.

It was easy to dance with Jason, as he was a principal dancer in the Hartford Ballet. He had danced in the Spoleto Festival in Italy, and right before Jack died, he returned from a seven-week tour performing leading roles in all the great opera houses of Central and South America. But he changed after that, gave up dancing and took construction jobs, even though the Joffrey Ballet was calling for him weekly. He had worked all his life for a ballet career, and suddenly he quit just when it was going so well. I didn't understand anything anymore.

A few days later I returned solo to Rhinestones 'n' Rawhide. I gathered up all of my courage to push myself to go after work. None of my friends was interested in dancing at a cowboy bar, and anyway I knew I had to learn to do things alone. At night, too. After all, I tried to console myself as I drove down Wilton Avenue to the Santa Monica Freeway, I went to Paris alone. I had learned a proverb in my French class: *La faim pousse le loup dans le village*: Hunger forces the wolf into the village.

The dry run with Jason had helped. Now I felt

THE CHURCH OF TANGO

comfortable in faded French jeans, a white denim sleeveless top with a low neck and built-in underwire bra, black leather belt with silver trim, and black bikers boots. I made myself walk in head high and breasts out as if I owned the place. And from that moment on, I pretty much did.

Rhinestones 'n' Rawhide sprawled through three bars, two practice floors, the central dance floor, and a pool room, with booths all around the perimeter. I soon learned that the regulars "hang" at designated locations, just as on high school campuses different groups congregate at certain places.

I joined the group by the elevated dance floor, where eight bar stools covered in fake black and white cowhide served as a cloak room. In the winter, layers of coats four and five deep covered the backs of the stools.

Being a regular was like being in an exclusive club or like going to a friend's house to a party every night. "Look who's with Barbara!" "Where have you been, haven't seen you in a while?" "Great outfit. Is it new?" "I've met someone..."

If we were a society, it was of lonely people. For we were all hungry to connect, if only for a moment. A few searched for a committed relationship, but most wanted the illusion of a social life—with the benefit of touching people of the opposite sex with no strings attached. It was easy to feel fulfilled after an evening of talking, laughing and dancing with your arms around someone.

It was strictly hand and arm touching only, however. The code of country dancing insisted on plenty of space between the couple. Books codifying the rules of country-dance etiquette were for sale at the door. It was sometimes hard to know if a "rule" was serious, like the division of the dance floor into concentric circles with the outside lane being the fast lane, or a put-on, like the exact relative dimensions of a cowboy's hat. ("Never touch a cowboy's hat without first asking permission!" was a serious rule.) Dress codes divided the proper looks into Country-Ballroom Style, Country-Western Style, and Yuppie Style, with the most important feature of them all being that one's jeans were long enough to "stack" over riding boots.

The rules also stated that it was a man's world on the dance floor. As for me, I loved not having to think. For the time I was at R & R my brain could take a holiday. I had no responsibility; for once I did not have to be in control. The man had to lead me. He had to plan the moves and run interference in traffic. For me, this two-steppin' was simple. I could naturally feel what to do from the music. If my partner led well, I could do anything with him.

The line dances were different. For these, people danced a set choreography, doing the same steps and turning in the same direction while packed in tight horizontal lines. There was no touching, except by accident. If someone didn't know a particular dance they often got hurt on the floor as a lot of the boots had steel toes. Because people essentially danced alone in line dancing, they often used this opportunity to show themselves off. The colored lights were turned up high overhead and the watchers with drinks and cigarettes in their hands squeezed closer to the floor to get a better look at the sexy girls who made a point of dancing in front, sometimes kicking high over the beer bottles sitting on the rail, flashing their underwear. The men were not immune to exhibiting themselves either, and would sometimes modify certain steps to include getting down on one knee and waving their cowboy hats, the Country-Ballroom guys wearing white jeans to show up in the spotlights.

People by and large learned and followed the rules. Sometimes when they didn't, fights broke out. Usually I was home by then.

———

There were three kinds of people who went to Rhinestones 'n' Rawhide: the dancers, the daters, and the drinkers. I was a dancer. All my life I had been a dancer, studying ballet since I was three and later modern jazz, then majoring in Dance at UCLA. Years later as a soloist, I joined Anthony Shay's AVAZ, a professional international folk dance company. A short time later I became artistic director and choreographer of my own cabaret dance troupe, which combined ballet and jazz with ethnic dance, and we toured California and did shows in Las Vegas, conventions, hotels, and annual concerts. In the last several years of raising a family and caring for my dying husband, I had forgotten how much I enjoyed dancing and how good I was at it. Now I realized, although maybe too late, that dancing was what I knew and did best, the only time I was one hundred percent confident.

The C & W music, which up until recently had sounded hokey and corny, now spoke to my newly awakened emotions, and the words—plaintive, sad, funny—communicated real human feelings, my own feelings. Some of the songs were hauntingly beautiful, achingly poignant.

My father had played country music on his guitar when I

was growing up, but in those days I didn't appreciate "Your Cheatin' Heart" and "The Tennessee Waltz." As a child I wished my father played other types of music, classical or even popular, instead of sitting in with the bands at the Palomino Club, then an L.A. cowboy dive, years later a cool and in vogue "scene." Now I reckoned this music must have been in my blood all along. It was too bad my father had not lived long enough to see me dancing to his kind of music every single night.

Rhinestones 'n' Rawhide seemed to appeal to everyone. I was sure that if I sat there long enough, everyone I ever knew would walk through the front door. I saw people there I had not seen since high school. I danced with movie stars and music celebrities, authentic cowboys in L.A. for a rodeo or on vacation from Wyoming or Montana, once even a Native American in buckskin, along with people from all over the world.

If there was a dancer's high to be had in that club, I would find it. I went Thanksgiving, Christmas, New Year's, my birthday, Easter Sunday, and the Fourth of July. My cowboy boots might just as well have been the Red Shoes.

CHAPTER 6

THE PRISONER POLKA

*"Home" is any four walls
that enclose the right person.*

~ Helen Rowland, U.S. journalist.
Reflections of a Bachelor Girl, (1903)

The morning of Jack's memorial service one week after his death, friends, parishioners, business associates, golfing and tennis buddies packed Hollywood Lutheran Church. There wasn't a dry eye as a gospel singer sang "Amazing Grace." The boys spoke and I did too, and the pastor gave a moving, heartfelt eulogy; he had known Jack since the day we met, married us, and knew what a good, and gentle man he was. My mother, whose "forgetfulness" was getting worryingly bad, kept asking as she looked around the church, "But where is Jack? He should be here." All 200 guests went over to the house for lunch, and it was the kind of party Jack would have liked—all our friends, joking, laughing, eating, drinking, remembering. Several made offers to help should I need any.

When someone dies "too soon," there is usually less left behind, as he's had less time to build up an estate. Jack had life insurance, but it was only enough for the educational expenses of the kids. He was too young to have accumulated much Social Security. He said to me after the diagnosis and terrible prognosis, "Cherie, you have to sell the house. That will be your fortune."

But I put off listing my "dream house," a comfortable old Spanish near the Hollywood Sign in the Los Feliz District that Jack and I had bought before we were married when the market was low. I had lived there longer than anyplace else in my life, and it was the only time I had ever been completely happy. I had everything I ever wanted during those years—the love of a good man who I respected, exciting artistic children, family joy, wonderful social life, perfect vacations, luxury cars, antiques and collections, including this lovely house. Its arches and arcades, stained glass windows, fountain, and blooming bougainvillea and wisteria fed my hunger for beauty. We had added a pool, and remodeled and enlarged the 1936 gracious home over the years to make it comfortable for our family, and, we had hoped, one day for visiting grandchildren.

Now that Jack was gone though, it was the time to be realistic and to take his advice. To end the worrying about the plumbing or electrical emergencies or the annual termite swarming that continued despite the best efforts of Bug Begone Exterminators and several thousand dollars. Or paying the gardener and the pool man. It was time to stop missing the ghosts of the little boys who grew up there, of Yasmeen who spent the sixteen years of her feline life there, of the many guests at the festive parties, of my life with Jack beginning with our wedding in the living room in front of the fireplace.

Initially I had tried to hang on to it and as much of my old lifestyle as possible. Before Jack died I worked half-time at the library, but I was able to bump it up into a full-time position, and I thought I could manage that way. By the time I realized it was impossible, the bottom had dropped out of the real estate market. I knew I couldn't have everything, and with Jack gone, my life was simply working at the library and hibernating in my bedroom. The boys were off doing their own things. Now, since that transformative trip to Paris, I prefered to return to France whenever I could, and for that, I needed more money and fewer responsibilities.

After Jack's death, several lawsuits against his estate were filed—the last chance for anyone to profit from knowing kind, generous, gentle Jack, Counselor at Law. The only one that scared me was some trickery of old friends/clients for whom Jack had served on the board of directors for their printing business. I had thought they were my friends too, as we socialized together and went to Las Vegas in a group every New Year's. They had all sat right down in front at the memorial service.

Three weeks after the service, a registered letter arrived from a firm of Italian lawyers announcing a lawsuit against Jack's "estate," me really, to recoup a high-interest loan these clients had taken out for their business. The fact of having to deal with something so huge without Jack, and doing it alone, made my whole body shake. I couldn't even understand what was going on, let alone how to deal with it. Panicked, lost, and frightened, I couldn't get on the phone to one of our "friends" fast enough.

"Toby, what is going on, what's this lawsuit I've just now heard about?"

"Oh don't worry, it's nothing personal. As a formality,

Jack signed on a loan with the rest of us, and hey, now we sold our business, we've liquidated everything, and all of us are off to Arizona!"

"But that's impossible! Jack never took out any loan. And now they are suing me, ME! Jack's estate is only my house. Toby, I thought we were friends."

"Well, Cherie, sorry. Let the lawyers handle it. I'm leaving town next week."

"So you're taking the money and running—leaving me holding the bag?"

"We have to live too," he said, and hung up.

Checking with Jack's law partner didn't make me feel better. The claim was legitimate and the money lenders (one and the same as the Italian law firm) were going after the only person left in town with an asset—me, the only person who had never seen any of that loan, nor had my husband. The Italians were suing me for all that the house was worth, which at the time of Jack's death was quite a bit. Toby and his brother planned the whole thing when they heard Jack was going to die. They had taken out the loan and then sold their business, their houses, boats, cars, and all of their assets in California. They planned to start over in Arizona with the money from the loan, that now I was supposed to pay back with the house equity.

I noticed that now there was always a car parked across the street with one or two men inside. Were they watching the house? Were they watching me? Perhaps the phone was tapped too so I didn't talk about selling the house except in person. I became paranoid that the lenders wanted to keep their eyes on the prize. Even though the market value had dropped considerably, the house was still worth a hefty chunk of change.

I was afraid to let the plaintiff law firm know I was putting the house up for sale in case they could quickly put a lien on it, so I listed it exclusively with Larry, a local broker who I knew from church and who had attended the memorial, with the stipulation of no For Sale sign in front. I told him the truth about my situation.

Larry complained that without the sign or a multiple listing, it was hard to bring buyers. He had very few showings, and most of those were looky-loos who didn't seem like they could afford to live under a bridge. Sometimes Larry, a portly middle-aged man with a comb-over, would just drop in, his eyes searching the rooms nervously, even greedily.

"Don't worry, Cherie, I've got this," he would say, his normally florid face flushed more scarlet than ever. "The market is falling so we'll just keep dropping the price until we find a buyer. I know you're concerned about the monthly outgo, but leave it to me." He would scuttle out without ever looking me or the boys in the eyes.

As the asking price for the house dropped lower and lower, I got more alarmed. How would I manage if the money lenders took all of the equity? I had nothing else but my salary. We had no investments other than the half of the apartment in France. However, in going though Jack's papers in the den, I found an old line of credit that we had applied for years ago in case of emergency. I called the bank; it was still viable.

So I made a plan. I went to the bank to draw as much cash as possible at one time on the line of credit, and came home and stashed it in a secret compartment. I explained to the managers that I was remodeling the house and the workers wanted to be paid in cash. I went every other day to a different branch of the bank and did the same thing until the line of credit was used up.

This way, no matter what happened in escrow, I had my money out of the house, my nest egg, and this second mortgage would be paid back to the bank through escrow at the time of the sale before the scoundrels could attach any of it. I thought it brilliant.

When I had taken out all I could, I filled a paper shopping bag with bundles of bills and went with Nancy to a small independent bank in West Hollywood and applied for a safety deposit box in her name. We packed the box with cash, and put in a note saying, "If anything happens to me, Nancy Barnes, this money belongs to Jason and Adam Z.…..."

After many months, still there were no offers on the house. Finally Larry called me at work to say there was one— his! He was going to help me out and take it off my hands, his words. Which surely was his plan all along, once he was able to get the price down low enough and I was desperate enough. I was desperate, and I accepted his offer.

The Italian lawyer/money lenders wrote me an angry letter that they were surprised there was no equity in the house, and demanded $25,000 to settle. I was afraid of them, and so I paid it.

I knew right away where I would move when escrow closed, to a tower in Park La Brea in West Hollywood. There were eighteen towers in all, plus a myriad of low-rise garden apartments clustered around the manicured parks and gardens. The community was fenced and gated and I had never been

THE CHURCH OF TANGO

inside the complex, though I had driven by it all of my life, usually on my way to Farmers' Market at Third and Fairfax. Now I wanted to live on the top of one of those towers; it had to be as unlike living in my old Spanish courtyard-style house as any place could be and that was what appealed to me. I could tolerate no pale imitation of my previous life.

The big house and yard sale was in full swing with dozens of people looking, handling, buying years of accumulated possessions of a family, when Jason left his post as security guard to bargain with a Russian couple over Jack's leather easy chair and hassock.

"I give you hundred dollars."

"Are you kidding me?" Jason was furious. "It's like new and it cost $1500!" He turned to me almost in tears. "Mom, can't I have this? We can't just give it away." Jason was always the sentimental one, who kept everything as souvenirs, who treasured his "home" more than anyone. He was bitter about my selling the house, and extremely angry with Larry. He wanted to keep everything because of all the happy memories, but he wanted the leather chair because it was so comfortable—and it had been Jack's.

"I wish you and Adam could hang on to more of our family things, but you have no place to put them now that you'll be bunking with Benny, and Adam doesn't want anything now that he's in that "fellowship," and anyway, we need the money. If you can get him up to $300, sell it."

Then I added, "If only you or Adam could take Great Grandma's wedding china… I so wish you both were settled now that we're moving."

"Mom, you should have had a girl." Neither Adam nor Jason unfortunately were in positions to keep china, silver, art work, furniture and antiques. We all had to do what we had to do, however painful. A daughter might have been able to somehow store a Bavarian china service for twelve, but two bachelor sons with no place of their own had more to worry about. The truth was that I would have liked us to somehow stay together, but Adam already had ties to this "group," and I felt that Jason needed to become more independent. In American society it wasn't healthy for a young man to live with his mother. Maybe I had made a mistake to send them as young teenagers to art schools across the country, but I couldn't turn back the clock now, as much as I wished to.

An Armenian woman was opening my parlor grand piano and I quickly moved to her side to say, "The piano is not for sale."

She insisted, "How much? Not worth much." She opened the petitpoint covered piano bench that my grandmother had made.

"It is not for sale!" I said, almost pushing her away. She gave up on the piano, letting the top of the bench fall down with a slam, but then went to a closet and opened it, inspecting its contents.

Larry showed up but refused to buy the custom drapery treatments or the unique fireplace screen and other items especially made for the house. He was more interested in measuring walls and checking out the basement. His family would be moving into the house the following week.

Buyers were still coming, even after the announced closing time, and I let them in to spend their money. They swept through the house, garage, and patio like vacuum cleaners, sucking up boxes of things in the back of the garage I had never seen, and attempting to buy the library books I had hidden in a closet. The only time I had difficulty was when a young couple bought the inlaid mahogany armoire from Belgium that could not fit into the Park La Brea apartment. I started to cry to see it being carried out the door; Jack had kept all his clothes in it. I soon cheered up after realizing that the five hundred dollars I made from the armoire was the price of a round-trip ticket to Paris. There was no question in my mind that I needed a trip to France more than an armoire.

By the time I took down the flags strung between the For Sale, SOLD! sign and the bougainvillea, it was dark, and everyone had left wearily. Adam was moving up to the mountains outside of Sacramento, Jason to friend Benny's, me to Park La Brea, and Larry and his family to this house.

Park La Brea was a surreal maze of one-way streets, traffic circles and look-alike buildings. Although I was paying for a parking space in an enclosed garage, I lived there almost a month before I had the time and energy to find it. In the beginning after I first moved in and came home late every night from dancing at Rhinestones 'n' Rawhide, I would just circle around and around the grounds until I found a free spot on one of Park La Brea's private streets. Then, when out of the car and alone in the dark, I often was disoriented and couldn't tell which of the identical towers was mine. Once I went up the elevator all thirteen floors of the wrong building. I got used to first checking the mailboxes in the lobby for my name. If it was not there, I trudged to the next tower through the park in my mini-skirt and cowboy boots.

At least I was not afraid to walk alone in the dark complex. If it was difficult for me to find my way, it must be for suspicious odd personages, too, because I never saw any. It was hard to find your way in, and even harder to get out. I felt like Patrick McGoohan's character, Number 6, from the sixties' paranoid cult TV series, "The Prisoner." Number 6 was a secret agent with amnesia who was held captive in a timeless British hamlet known only as "The Village." All traces of his previous existence were erased by the mindbenders in control of this post-Kafka nightmare fantasy. In each episode Number 6 tried in vain to escape from the beautiful, quaint and seemingly peaceful "Village."

Each night returning "home" by going up in an elevator brought down around my head an opaque cloud of loneliness and depression. I missed my house but was glad to be out from under the responsibilities of a home-owner. Park La Brea had a fabulous location right in the middle of Hollywood and close to work, and the price was right for the large amount of space I rented. I kept as much of my furniture as I could so I needed a big space to put it in. If I had any maintenance problem, all it took was a phone call. Even my Hoosier cabinet fit into the kitchen. But it was strange for a native Angelina not to pull her car up directly in front of her front door, the freedom of the L.A. Way of Life that was so familiar to me. I kept telling myself I'd get used to it. Somehow the confines of the labyrinthine streets and the elevator and the concrete tower I lived in made me an actual prisoner. It always seemed like forever before I could make my escape onto Third Street, and I would chant Number 6's mantra in frustration: "I will not be pushed, filed, stamped, indexed, briefed, debriefed or numbered! My life is my own!"

One late night I picked up my mail and stood in the lobby in front of the bank of mailboxes, stunned. There was a letter from Olivier among the catalogs and bills in my hand. I had answered his note months ago, and he replied now? He enclosed his picture, a goofy photo of him with a pigeon on his head, his black hair curling all around his face. He wrote on the back in French: "Sorry to be so late in wishing you Happy New Year. Kisses. Olivier."

So he hadn't forgotten me.

CHAPTER 7

FRENCH APPEAL

*Sex appeal is fifty percent what you've got
and fifty percent what people think you've got.*

~ Sophia Loren

I couldn't get weighed down here and now, I realized. I must experience things other than those in my back yard. Somehow I had to make my dream come true to live in Paris. I went back to French school, but this time in Los Angeles. Tuesdays I went late to dance at Rhinestones 'n' Rawhide because after work I drove over to Westwood and the beautiful UCLA campus, my old alma mater where I felt so at home.

Professeur Raymond asked, "Alors, where are you from?"

"I was born here in L.A., pourquoi?"

"I was wondering why you have a Belgian accent."

Evidently I had sung along with Jacques Brel too much in the car.

In UCLA's weekly Conversational French, Professeur Raymond assigned oral "exposés" on any topic. Students talked about French politics, their past global travels, their own hometowns, the French Resistance in World War II. One woman made a large chart to present "tous les hommes de ma vie," all the men in her life.

For my presentation I brought a cassette player and photocopies of the words to Jacques Brel's song, "Mon Enfance." After explaining a little about Brel's life and art, I talked about the meaning of the "poetry" of his work and then read aloud his lyric/poem about growing up in Belgium, feeling alien in a world that did not understand him, waiting to get on a train that never comes. When I played the tape of Brel singing his autobiographical song, the class sat silent after the final arpeggio.

"Do you know about Charles Aznavour? Have you heard his recordings? If you're familiar with Brel and Montand, now you must also know Aznavour," Raymond told me.

"Is he as good? No one can possibly be." When I liked someone, I really liked them.

"Yes, he's good, but different. Neither is ethnically French—Brel was Belgian, Aznavour is Armenian—but they became quintessential French popular singers and songwriters. Tiens, I think he'll be in town next week on tour. You should go. In fact, the whole class should go!"

For our fieldtrip Raymond was able to get the class a block of seats in the sixth row at the Doolittle Theater on Vine Street in Hollywood. When the orchestra began a jazzy tune with lots of brass, the curtain went up on the empty stage, and a very small dark man in a brown suit and narrow tie strode out from the wings.

> *Laisse--moi guider tes pas dans l'existence,*
> *Laisse-moi la chance de me faire aimer…*
> *Le Temps, le temps, le temps et rien d'autre.*

I was mesmerized. This man was short, old—at least twenty years my senior—balding and homely, yet he was so sexy. He sang with purpose and energy about all aspects of romantic love: young love, old love, married love, suffering love, the beginning of love, the ending of love. He sang like he really understood what love was all about. What could a woman find more appealing than that?

His small body was graceful and his large hands expressive. The vibrato in his voice caused me to imagine things he could do with his mouth and tongue. I was certain he was a magnificent lover. Suddenly I was so hot; I was sweating hard and took off my blazer in the air-conditioned hall.

"La Bohème" was a crowd favorite I could tell, as the applause started with the first notes of the waltz from the piano. He sang of nostalgia in looking back on Bohemian artist days in Paris when the singer and his beauteous nude model were poor, in love, and foolish but happy, because they were young. At the end of the song, the orchestra played faster and Aznavour pantomimed an artist painting at his easel, wiping his pretend brush with his real white handkerchief. The violins tore on with a passion, then the music stopped, the handkerchief was thrown to the floor—and the lights went out. Not a heartbeat later three women climbed on stage and fought over the scrap of white fabric.

"That always happens," Raymond whispered to me. "They wait for it at each performance."

I had never wanted Elvis' silk scarf, but now I wanted Aznavour's handkerchief. I wondered if it smelled of cologne, if he deliberately scented it in his dressing room before tucking it into his jacket pocket, thinking of the woman who would later take it home to put under her pillow.

I marveled how someone not very physically attractive could be so appealing. After all, Brel, too, was almost ugly, physically. What perfect examples of how beauty and sex appeal come from within. Maybe being French didn't hurt.

⁓

With the holidays approaching, I really pushed myself to go to R & R, knowing that people and dancing were good for me. I was bone-tired, soul-tired, but still I got ready with blush and mascara, silver earrings and cowboy boots. How could I stay in my cold, disorganized and out-of-control apartment on the top floor of a complex out of science fiction? Going "home" each time was like going to a foreign country. I didn't like living alone; I missed my sons and most of all, Jack. I felt more at home on the streets of Paris than I did in my own apartment in Park La Brea.

If I arrived at the club before 7:00 p.m. I got in free. Plus there was a Happy Hour complimentary buffet until 8:00. I never drank anything but ice water, for which I tipped the bartenders $2. My work day ended at 5:30, I ran home to change, and got to R & R by 6:30, ate a couple of chicken wings, danced my heart out, and was home by 10:00.

People who watched me at Rhinestones 'n' Rawhide must have thought I was a maniac. I danced like someone possessed. I didn't know where the energy came from. Instead of one hip bump I did five, a simple grape-vine step became a complicated choreographed total body—feet, hips, shoulders, head, pelvis, torso—ballet. I watched myself with my mind's eye and I saw an energy burst, super-turbo manic woman flailing away by herself as if her life depended on it. I probably looked ridiculous to be moving everything God gave me in public in time to the music at my age. I guessed that was out of control too. Dancing was the only thing I was good at. I was out of the loop while dancing, that's all I knew. When I couldn't find a "horseshow" partner, I danced alone in the center of the floor. No one was after my bandanna, but the club manager asked me to fill in teaching group classes before the regular dancing started. "Sure," I said, "I'll be teaching in Paris at my own club one day soon."

CHAPTER 8

HOLIDAY AT DU-PAR'S

Try to be a more happy person

~ The Dalai Lama

The answering machine was blinking like crazy Christmas Eve after work. There were six messages, all from friends canceling plans we had made for Christmas Day: a sister's unexpected visit, an invitation from a daughter's boyfriend's family, Nancy had a last-minute chance to go out of town. I didn't expect to hear from Adam or Jason because I already knew they had other plans. I think they wanted to avoid Christmas and the pangs of memories just like I did.

I changed into my dancing clothes and went to Normandie Towers Retirement Home in Hollywood, where I ate a lasagna dinner with my mother and the other old folks in the communal dining room decorated with plastic wreaths and foil Stars of David. I missed my mother, even when we were together like tonight. We had always been so close, such good friends. She was flakey and ditsy and stubbornly independent, and somehow she could always sense the truth of a situation. She wasn't highly educated, she was the only one in her family to graduate from high school, even with her health issues. But she knew things and she read me like a book. My wise intuitive mother and I had talked over everything and confided in one another. She had been forbidden to get pregnant because of a congenital heart condition. When it accidentally happened, her doctors wanted to give her an abortion, saying she would never live through a birth. She refused, risking death to have me. She told me that even if she were to die, she would have that baby. What a brave decision when she had been told all her life that she couldn't survive pregnancy and childbirth. She was forbidden to roller skate or to ride a bicycle. She had been forced to stay in bed for a year when she was eighteen. What went on in her head during those nine months of pregnancy when every one was trying to convince her to terminate? Did she wake every morning fearing that day would be her last? What she told me was that she never felt better in her life.

Now that intimate, confidential part of our relationship was over, destroyed by Alzheimer's. Tonight we could only talk about the food and the small worries Mom could find words for. She didn't even know it was Christmas. I was heartsick lonely for the person sitting right next to me.

Then I went dancing.

Everyone there tonight will be either friendless or Jewish, I thought as I headed south on Arlington to the freeway, noting the leafless trees speeding past me in the dark and all the closed businesses lit with forlorn strings of colored lights. I whispered that thought later at Rhinestones 'n' Rawhide to one of my dance partners, adding, "I'm friendless. Which are you?" He replied, "I'm Jewish!" and our peals of laughter accompanied our two-stepping around the almost empty dance floor. I was home by eleven-forty-five and in bed by midnight, purposely avoiding midnight Mass on the media.

My emotions bounced around so. One minute I was confident, and the next insecure. One minute I was positive about the future, the next scared shitless. One minute I was energetic, the next tired as hell. I didn't feel in control anywhere but on the dance floor. When I danced I felt beautiful, secure, happy, connected, and powerful. Most of all, when I danced I felt like myself. It was addictive.

The next afternoon I got up and went across the street to Farmer's Market to have "Christmas dinner" at the counter of Du-Par's Coffee Shop. The place was jammed, but outside of the occasional elderly couple and divorced fathers trailing holiday-custody children, everyone was alone.

The bright Southern California winter sun glanced off the low windows, shining on the emptiness of the closed Farmer's Market, and filling the warm and crowded dining room. The majestic San Gabriel Mountains far away were clearly visible. Earthquake weather, my mother would have called it.

Du-Par's, a hospitable island of food and warmth in an ocean of holiday loneliness in West Hollywood, was the only available place to eat today for miles around. Maybe because of that and the Muzak Christmas songs and all the red and green balloons tied to the wooden booths, a spirit of camaraderie somehow prevailed. All of us had that one thing in common, we had nowhere else to go for Christmas dinner, or else why were we there?

The people sitting at the horseshoe-shaped counter were telling jokes to one another while the waitresses served as moderators and talk-show hosts. I contributed a news item I had just heard on the radio, that people who drink coffee are less depressed.

That inspired a white-bearded man a few stools away to tell the story of Frenchman Antoine Robidoux who aided the American cause in California during the Mexican War. Robidoux, severely wounded in battle and near death, was awakened during the freezing night by the smell of coffee. "Eef onlee I can 'ave a cup of zhat precious brew, my life it will be zaved," said the bearded man, giving this line his best Hollywood French accent. The story went on to relate that Robidoux's comrade tracked down the coffee being heated over a nearby campfire, and poured it into the failing body of his friend, who promptly revived. Voilà!

The Du-Par's coffee-drinkers applauded and raised our cups in a toast to the power of our favorite beverage. The waitresses thought we all needed refills, and scurried around dispensing the life and hope-giving brew from steaming stainless-steel pots like priests celebrating Mass.

I loved to sit at a certain section of the counter because of Sophie, who called me and all of her other customers Honey and Dear Heart. She was the quintessential wisecracking American coffee-shop waitress. Admitting to being seventy-two years old, she must have earned a lot in tips but could have cleaned up in stand-up comedy. Sophie, besides having great gray hair on which sat the requisite ridiculous tiny hat, and lots of energy, was never at a loss for a joke, witty repartee, funny comments. Eating in her section was like participatory dinner theatre in which people joined in with jokes of their own and everyone laughed as a group.

Wouldn't it be fun if we all wore name tags, they brought out bottles of champagne, and we could have our own Christmas party of lonely strangers! Or maybe we weren't lonely after all. Here we were on a bright California day in December, eating and laughing around a table with a great hostess. How bad was that?

That night I went dancing.

CHAPTER 9

THE KEY

There are thoughts which are prayers.
There are moments when,
whatever the posture of the body,
the soul is on its knees.

~ Victor Hugo

My old next-door neighbors, Linda and Steve, were still my friends. Most of the others had fled when Jack had gotten sick, either out of fear of cancer and death, or displeasure at my being a single woman who made social arrangements awkward. Whatever the reason, my old circle of friends was gone.

One of my fondest memories had been a special group of six friends who used to do everything together—trips, restaurants, concerts, our children's performances and graduations. We all dined outdoors by the pool at our house almost weekly in the summer. The patio light would shine on the six of us in the dark backyard as we ate Jack's barbeque, drank wine and laughed. I never laughed as much as with Jack, Francesca, Bill, Mary, and Khaled. The teasing, good-natured sarcasm, remembrances of old adventures we had together, wacky schemes and plans, the interplay of our six very different personalities. I felt so happy and blessed, so lucky, so secure in that bright circle of beloved friends—all gone now, along with Jack, to different places for different reasons.

But Linda and Steve included me still from time to time in gatherings and I loaned them the occasional use of my French apartment.

After moving to Park La Brea, it was difficult to drive through my beautiful old neighborhood of Los Feliz where I had lived since I was twenty years old. It was painful to be where it still felt like home but no longer was, to drive towards the beacon of the Griffith Park Observatory and not to arrive home. Regret bloomed especially heavy in March when the Indian tababuia trees planted up and down the street as a neighborhood project were in full pink blossom.

When I went to visit Linda and Steve, there was no choice but to park under the tababuia trees, and of course I would stare at my old house, breathing in the intense aroma of the cedar tree next door and the night blooming jasmine I had put in the front yard years ago. Being so close to Griffith Park and Fern Dell, there was always a fresh, cool scent of the forest and the historic Cedars of Lebanon trees lining Los Feliz Boulevard. The old house now looked just the same as always and I had the fantasy that behind the locked wrought-iron gates to the courtyard, and behind the cozy lighted windows, was my old life. The drawn draperies glowed from within like a candle in the window lit for me.

That if I only still had the key, if I could just get in, it all would be there: Jack, alive and full of good humor and health, the little boys watching TV and making mischief, my mother over for dinner, Yasmeen the cat sleeping on the bed, and all of my treasured antiques and collections. If I had the key, I could open the door to see Yasmeen waiting for me in the hallway with the kids' musical instrument cases piled next to the stairs, Adam playing his horn in the living room with his friends, Jack watching football, Jason working out, my mother warming up the pot of split pea soup she brought over for dinner, the phone ringing off the hook, a stack of mail waiting on the hall tree that was more than catalogs and bills.

Maybe if I stared long and hard enough through the bright and golden windows, I could catch the shadow of my vanished life, the comings and goings of a happy family.

What if I found the key and opened the door into another dimension and came home?

CHAPTER 10

DISCO AT THE BATHS

Dance first.
Think later.
It's the natural order.

~ Samuel Beckett

Paris was still there, just as I had left it last winter on my first solo trip a year ago. Lately I had been dreaming about France, and Olivier, and sometimes in the mornings while driving to work I wondered if I had not made it all up. My Paris reawakening lived in my head like a fantasy. And now here I was once again in the shadow of elegant architecture, glorious history, and hope. Rhinestones 'n' Rawhide, lawsuits, Park La Brea were a world away—at least for two weeks.

I delayed a day before going to the rue Saint Honoré. Then, one late afternoon I took a sidewalk table at the tabac across the street from the school and waited for Olivier to walk through the blue double doors on his way home. I wanted to be discreet and not to make him uncomfortable in any way. Above all I wanted to keep him as a friend and not risk alienating him. Going directly to the school to see him seemed too brash and forward under the full glare of his colleagues. I was sure that he had had many students with crushes on him before, but I was trying hard not to act like a silly schoolgirl, what the French call a *midinette*. I had dropped him a postcard saying I'd be in Paris for these two weeks but left it vague.

I nursed my tiny espresso long past the time it had grown cold. I too was freezing as I sat at one of the tables on the sidewalk, dark beginning to fall. I knew that somehow I had missed him.

The next day I was less subtle. Again at Madame de Chardon's because I knew what to expect, the excellent location, and the price was right, I rose early and avoided her miserable instant breakfast by saying I was on a diet. Her apartment was exactly the same as before and I felt at home in the bright pink bedroom. I took the Métro to the Tuileries and walked to the café where we had our first drink together last February. I knew, because I had looked him up in the phone book and on the map, that Olivier must pass by there on his way to work in the mornings. And so I installed myself in a corner window, ordered café au lait, and waited. Like a stalker.

At last I saw his familiar backpack, jacket and cloud of curly black hair as he loped down the street. Once again like last winter, I ran after him.

"Olivier! Bonjour! Comment vas-tu?" I couldn't help flashing my big American smile. I was just so happy to see him again.

We made plans to lunch together, and over hot goat cheese salads, croque-monsieur sandwiches and tastes of unfamiliar dishes that he offered me on his fork from his plate, the conversation became more personal and intimate than it had been last year.

He confided that he was writing his memoirs, and when my eyes lit up, he brought a portfolio of the loose pages at our next lunch. "I would be interested to know what you think of my writing," he said, and of me, he implied. I accepted the manuscript like a gift.

After a private French lesson with last year's professeur, Nathalie, at her apartment, I walked down the rue de Belleville to the Métro station at the bottom of the hill, the odors of a dozen cultures assaulting my senses: Chinese herbs, Arabic spices, exotic fruits in the open air stalls, cooking smells from Asian restaurants and Kosher delicatessens, and as everywhere in Paris, the warm yeasty fragrance of baking bread. Belleville was one of the oldest neighborhoods in the city and in recent years was the most culturally diverse, the crowded streets full of tall and graceful Africans elegant as kings and queens in their flowing colorful robes.

Just like last year's solo trip, I didn't feel like a visitor to Paris, but at home. And now I felt superior to "ordinary" tourists, as I knew just how to balance on the balls of my feet as the Métro rocked to a stop and how to move with confidence in the right direction on the quai without having to look up at the Sortie and Correspondance signs. I also learned at last what were the rolled up carpets laying in the gutters at street corners everywhere. Last February I could only figure they were lost bedrolls of the homeless, but now I knew they were a part of the street cleaning and drainage system, as iconoclastic in a modern city as the twig brooms the cleaners used, now manufactured from green plastic, but twigs nevertheless. I also discovered the source of the mysterious flashes constantly emanating from the top of the Eiffel Tower at night: the automatic flashes on the cameras of tourists. Knowing these details were small victories to me. To the French, you don't have to be born in Paris to be a Parisian, or even born in France, you just must live in Paris. And now, for a few days, I felt Parisienne, an unknown, life-long craving at last satisfied.

I bought all the Aznavour, Montand and Brel cassettes I could find at FNAC in Les Halles. Unable to resist the concert videos I saw displayed on the street, I bought those too, even though they were incompatible with American VCR's. I watched them at Elizabeth's and Jean-Luc's when I went to visit them, transfixed by Brel's performances. Energy and sweat rolled off Brel in performance. Short, teeth too big, huge hands and graceful body, I understood why no other artists performed his songs, why he was unique, and perhaps why he burned himself out so young.

I hunted out their biographies and critiques in bookstores, and bought sheet music of their songs, longing to make the music a part of me by playing it on the piano.

I also checked out the crazy possibility of opening a cowboy dance club in Paris. I actually went to see some properties for lease, but they were too small or had zoning restrictions on noise. Bernard, the realtor I had met at Elizabeth's party suggested a barge moored in the river, so I canvassed up and down the Seine, looking for péniches with A Vende signs, sketching floorplans in my French notebook. I could live on the boat in the cabin, and make an indoor dance floor and one on the top deck as well in the open air, with a bar on each deck. One corner would be a boutique selling CDs and western clothing. And we would serve American-style snacks: chili, tacos, spareribs, hot wings, hamburgers. I even picked out the name: "Cherie's Bus Stop," after the popular 1956 Joshua Logan movie starring Marilyn Monroe, which the French honored as a cult film. Maybe I could even get Jason to work as a bouncer.

In my bathrobe, with Madame listening from across the room, I made a reservation for a table for one at Les Bains-Douches' upstairs restaurant, and then put on the sexiest clothes I had in my suitcase: a miniskirt over a plunging bodysuit. I wondered what Madame thought of all this as I called out "Au revoir" in answer to her, "Amusez-vous bien!"

Along with looking at barges and spaces for lease, I had spent the first few days of my stay going to galleries and museums, studying French with Nathalie, and having lunch with my new French friends, including Olivier. I had been hoping to find someone, Bernard for instance, to go with me to Les Bains Douches, the most famous and à la mode discothèque in the world. I wanted to see what a French dance club was like. In Paris the action did not even begin until midnight and then went until dawn, "jusqu'à l'aube" according to L'Officiel des Spectacles. And what did one do alone until then?

Bourgeoise and economical, Madame, in the bedroom slippers and rose chenille robe de chambre she always wore at home, padded into my pink room while I was readying myself in the bathroom, and turned off the lamp and unplugged my hair dryer. I already knew the curious old lady went through my drawers and nosed among my things, so I didn't really mind. After all what did I have to hide? It was even amusing to be the object of the landlady's prying; it was so different from living alone.

I walked down the hill in the rain to the empty taxi stand behind the church of Notre Dame de Lorette. I waited in the chilly and wet black night, and when there was no sign of a cab, continued walking through the dark until at last I spied one with an illuminated Taxi Parisian sign on its roof. The cab dropped me in front of the old Turkish bath on a small side street near Les Halles. All was quiet at Les Bains and I felt conspicuous as I climbed the front steps alone to confront the doorman, a mountain of a man dressed in white and black. I could see why the French slang for doorman was "gorille".

"Oui?" He looked me up and down.

"I have a reservation for dinner," I told him defiantly in French.

"Bien sûr, madame," and without even a hint of a smile he opened the red velvet rope, indicating another flight of stairs going up to the restaurant inside.

I felt naked under his gaze as I ascended the staircase and entered the Philippe Starck-decorated restaurant. There were a few occupied tables and a long zinc-topped bar running the length of the narrow room. No one was at the bar but the bartender, and since I didn't know what else to do, I went over and perched on one of the stools. It was obvious that at eleven-fifteen it was very early indeed.

"Un kir, s'il vous plaît," I said when the bartender approached.

A very young, very thin, very handsome man in a white jacket came up behind me. "You are having dinner, non?"

"Yes. I made a reservation. Magnus." I pronounced it the French way.

"Oh I regret, Madame, we are not yet set up for one. We have many large parties tonight. Please, you do not mind waiting a little?"

I did mind, I felt awkwardly on stage in the half-empty, quiet restaurant. There was no one else, man or woman, there alone.

The maitre d' brought another kir and the bartender set down a silver bowl of nuts and chips, and I continued to wait for my table for one. I watched beautiful models come in with their entourages, including their own photographers. After a few minutes I got used to the barrage of flashes that greeted each glamorous girl dressed in bare skin and black as she entered and posed for the photographers and everyone else in the room. Many people seemed to know each other, and greeted new arrivals flamboyantly with lots of kissing.

Finally a table was set for me, and I was shown to it with a great flourish. Once seated I felt less conspicuous and regarded the menu with pleasure, anticipating another delicious French meal. "Oui, salmon, salad, cheese, tarte aux poires, half bottle of white wine, half bottle of Evian."

Since I was squeezed shoulder to shoulder between two men at neighboring tables, soon we began to converse. The man on my right introduced himself as Gérard, and we chatted while he was having dinner with two other men.

"Paris is bored, bored with disco, the music, the dancing, tout. Par exemple, my friends and I came tonight only to dine. We are not going down to dance at all. We just find the restaurant très sympa." At this his eyes followed a tall blond in a tiny black leather miniskirt and thigh-high boots as she swept into the room. It was Claudia Schiffer. I wondered if his comments meant tout Paris would be open for something completely different—maybe a cowboy dance club?

By the time I signaled for the check the restaurant was filling up. It was one in the morning, and I could not put off any longer descending the two flights of stairs to the basement discotheque. A smaller space than I expected, the tiles and mosaics of the old public bathhouse were barely visible behind the crush of people and the heavy veil of cigarette smoke.

There was no way to tell where the dance floor began. People were moving to the loud repetitive disco beat in the center of standees stacked five or six deep around the wall, with smaller rooms filled with couches and easy chairs at each side of the main bar and dance area. Conversation was impossible due to the high-decibel beat, but everyone was doing what he or she came there to do, to see and be seen.

Maybe a Paris branch of Rhinestones 'n' Rawhide could replace the ennui of disco! The French were crazy about any and everything cowboy. Trendy shops had names like Cowboy Bleu and The Far West, and stylish young people wore jeans and fringed leather jackets with western boots. There were cowboy bars with live bands imported from the States, and a country radio station. Perhaps a C & W dance club on the banks of the Seine really could be my ticket to living in France. The cash in the safety deposit box was burning a hole in my future.

Downstairs in the old tiled baths, hands were busy with

drinks and cigarettes, faces expressionless or looking bored, no one appeared to be having much fun. More people were dancing alone than with someone, it being more important to show off than meet people. I would have left sooner if I could have figured out gracefully where the exit was, hidden as it was behind a velvet curtain.

And so I was unprepared when a tall man made his way over to me from across the room. "May I buy you another of what you are drinking?" he asked in French. Due to the loud music and my surprise I didn't understand at first. He was well dressed, nice-looking, with a sweet face, and so I accepted a gin and tonic. Even though conversation was virtually hopeless, I noticed that we quickly passed to the familiar verb conjugation, and "tutoyer"-ed each other before I finished my cocktail. We danced a little, and when he finally leaned down to put his lips against my ear and ask if it wasn't time to go to his place, it felt natural to nod yes, but I didn't.

"Merci," I said and kissed him on the cheek as I grabbed my bag and slid off my stool, making my way through the curtain, up the stairs, and out into the night, spotting a taxi appearing out of the gloom.

"Cherie, is that you?" The next day chez Madame it was Nancy calling on the phone from L.A. "I hate to ruin your vacation, but your mother fell out of bed and broke her wrist! She's in the hospital, and needs surgery. You have to sign papers and everything. And I guess your mother is pretty upset and confused. Can you come home?"

My poor mother. I had given Nancy's phone number to the retirement home in case of emergency. There was no other family to call on, only Adam or Jason, and they were having a very hard time with their grandmother's Alzheimer's. She was my responsibility. I had to be with her.

The first available flight was not until the next day, I called Steve and Linda at their Paris hotel to see if I could join them for dinner that night. I needed to be with someone, and who better than old friends from Los Angeles. But Steve said that he and Linda wanted their last dinner in Paris to be alone, and that he knew I would understand. I didn't understand. They lived alone in L. A. and they had been alone on their entire trip to France. They had stayed free in my Evian apartment alone for the last ten days. Linda knew I was in trouble, she heard me crying on the phone. I didn't understand what friends were for, if when you really needed them they wouldn't help you. Or who was really your friend at all.

I thought about my mother being alone and frightened and not understanding what was going on. Like me, in a way. After watching Jack die in intense physical pain with his mind completely about him, and watching my mother die of an evil, mind-rotting disease causing psychic pain of huge dimensions, I didn't know which was worse. Jack knew he would die, my mother couldn't remember much but knew what Alzheimer's meant. Perhaps the loss of one's mind was the ultimate personal horror, more tragic than death.

CHAPTER 11

DANCING TIL IT HURTS

Dancing participants, fearful of dying; would work themselves into an hysterical frenzy, screaming and convulsing in an effort to sweat the disease from the body.

~ T.C. Campbell, Dance Mania of the Middle Ages

Mom looked small and forlorn in someone else's sweatshirt and slippers, her right arm in a huge plaster cast as she sat in a chair in the Angel View Nursing Home's corridor. It was St. Patrick's Day and her name was printed on a green shamrock taped by the door to her room. Jason and I had written her name on all her clothes with a magic marker, but somehow she was never wearing them.

Two women were screaming elsewhere on the locked ward, one for her husband, the other out of pure fury, and big Charlie Parker leered at me as he slumped in a chair across the hall. Hasmik, the sweet Armenian lady, smiled as I walked down the hall past the woman who constantly folded and unfolded her bedclothes, and the man with a cane walking circles down the hall and around and around the bare concrete patio.

Mom started to cry when she saw me. "You've got to get me out of here. I can't stand another minute. I want to go back to my place. Is it still there?"

"Mom, you are talking real well today. Can you tell me your name?"

"I can't think..."

"Mommy, if you don't know your name," I said, trying hard to swallow the lump in my throat and to keep a reasonable tone of voice, "how can you go back to living alone? And what if you fell out of bed again and broke your hip the next time?" Deep inside, I knew it was useless to be logical. I tried to hug her, but she pushed me away.

She began to cry again. I glanced through the open door of her room and saw that her TV set still had no rabbit ears. Adam and I had brought it over from her apartment in the Normandie Towers retirement home, but it needed an antenna. Jason had said he'd take care of it, but that was a while ago. Maybe she couldn't understand the programs, but still it was something familiar and company to have it on. She used to be addicted to TV, never neglecting to watch her soap operas and talk shows. I noticed another visitor who sat with his father in front of the television, the son watching a ball game, the father staring out into space. At least it was a way to spend time together.

Mom would have to wear the big cast from her fingers to her shoulder for at least two months, which meant staying in the Angel View nursing home until then. The place was clean, but every inch an institution with a high-security Alzheimer's wing and gray-skinned patients in wheelchairs and bathrobes. There was not one thing about it that was a "home."

My red-haired Irish mother loved to dance, and to sing. My father had been an amateur musician who could play any instrument, so the two of them were always making and enjoying music during my childhood, at least until alcoholism completely owned my father. I resented him for that, but at least he was a "happy drunk," without a violent bone in his body. He was generous and fun-loving and liked nothing more than to invite folks over and feed them, usually with plenty of highballs, beer, and impromptu live music.

My parents sang in the church choir when they went, my dad in a barbershop quartet, my mom in the Sweet Adelines Chorus. There were frequent parties at our house where the live music and booze flowed all night. There was no way she could sit out "Up a Lazy River," or "You Made Me Love You." If there was one word to describe my mother, it was "fun." If you wanted someone to liven up your party, you invited Lee.

As my mother got older—and alone—she never neglected a senior citizen dance. Men loved her, right up to the end, even in the Alzheimer's wing, and at one time she herself might have been the Queen of the Stardust Ballroom on Sunset Boulevard in Hollywood where she lived.

She never forgot music, but she began to forget words. That was the first sign of her impending illness. She was diagnosed with Alzheimer's several years ago, when she couldn't draw the face of a clock, even though there was one on the wall right in front of her.

Word by word, the disease progressed slowly. She lived

on her own far longer than she should have, even continuing to drive every morning to the House of Pies for breakfast. The waitresses there took special care of her, and when she didn't remember what she wanted to eat, they knew and brought it to her anyway. When I or my sons wanted to find her in the morning, we went to the House of Pies, where invariably she, so bright and pretty and sweet, would be sitting at the counter nursing her coffee, happy as a canary.

Always feisty and self-sufficient, like so many others faced with the helpless doom of Alzheimer's, my mother had refused to give up her car and to move into a retirement home where meals were served and theoretically someone would keep an eye on her. She got angry every time the subject of leaving her apartment came up. Finally Adam and Jason removed the battery from her car in the parking garage. Their grandmother didn't know how to deal with that, didn't know how to call a mechanic or the Auto Club, so at last she was grounded.

No more worries about her running over a pedestrian with her big Pontiac, but we were still apprehensive about how she would eat and take care of herself. Maybe she would leave the stove on, or get lost on the street. Packets of jelly, butter, and sugar she brought home from the coffee shop littered her kitchen, but she forgot to eat them. She forgot how to use the TV's remote and forgot how to dial the phone. So the boys and I packed her up and moved her forcibly into the Normandie Towers Retirement Home, which the brochure claimed "was like being home with a loving family."

Mom didn't agree; she was furious. "If it weren't for this darned ole' Alzheimer's I could still be in my own place! I didn't want to come here but you made me move anyway." This was the first time I could remember my mother ever getting mad at me, but I felt better knowing she was better supervised, and that there was a nurse on call. The staff and other residents of Normandie Towers took to her and saw that she went to the dining room for meals on time. Or I had to trust that they did.

One night, after a false alarm and trip to the hospital for chest pains, when Jason and I got her back to Normandie Towers he left to buy her a sandwich as she had missed dinner. All of a sudden she became agitated, screaming as she sat on the bed and holding her head. Now it was I who was terrified. Though her cries and screams were loud, no one came to inquire. When I selected this place, the staff promised me that everyone was treated as family, that they looked out for one another. What bullshit.

When Mom was calm enough to talk, she told me how years ago a doctor had euthanized her mother—my grandmother—because she had the same condition of Alzheimer's. Mom had never told me this before, kept it to herself for forty years. "He just put her to sleep. He put a pillow over her head. And why oh why can't someone do that for me?" she asked.

———

The man who constantly bellowed in bewildered rage for his wife Stella started in when I was buzzed through the locked door of Angel View. I could hear this senile Stanley Kowalski even when I telephoned the nurses' station: "STELLA! STELLLLLAA!!!"

Another only pleaded, "Oh God, please take me!"

And why couldn't He? What had these people done to deserve their final years lived like this? I made a conscious effort to speak cheerfully to them and to look them in the eyes, where I of course saw my future self. I supposed Alzheimer's was in my genes too.

It was only six-thirty but almost every patient in the nursing home was already put to bed. Mom didn't remember I had been there earlier that day. It was her birthday, and there had been a cake and party hats in the dining room when I visited for lunch. "How old am I again?" she asked me sweetly. "Seventy-six? My, that's old, isn't it?"

Now she talked reasonably to me about the waste of money to keep her room at Normandie Towers. "I want to go back but I know I can't for a long time. But please, will you take me to see it?"

I was so ashamed that I didn't have the strength to take her. Aside from dealing with her reactions and emotions, I'd have to handle my own. And the thought of seeing her among all her funny and sweet old-lady possessions for probably the last time tore me apart.

The next time I visited she was waiting for me inside the locked doors, sweater in hand. "Let's go," she said.

"Go where?"'

"To my place, so I can talk to them about moving to a place lower down. I fell because my apartment was up too high." She couldn't make the connection in her brain that she fell out of bed, not out of her apartment on the sixth floor.

"I'm sorry, Mom, we can't go, not today. I have to go to work soon."

Angry now, she cried, "You hate me! I hate you too! Why are you so mean to me?" Tears streamed down her face and fell in splashes on the tile floor.

She was on a shower strike and would not clean up or change her clothes because she was waiting to go "home" to do it. My presence just seemed to enrage my mother, and besides I felt so helpless and upset to see her frantic, so I punched in the numbered code to unlock the door of the ward so I could leave. With that, my mom tried to push me away and to get out through the now open double doors, using the big heavy cast on her arm as a lever and a weapon. The other woman patient who was always banging on the door crying to get out, was ready to escape too.

I yelled for the nurse, who came running down the hall towards the commotion at the door. These poor people were like hamsters in a cage, using all their energy and wiles and waking hours trying to escape. Only hamsters usually succeed. These folks didn't have a chance.

When mom's roommate beat up the nurse trying to give her medication, and another patient shoved my mother violently to the floor, I campaigned to get her moved out of the Alzheimer's wing.

The "normal" patients in Angel View were less physically able, and in fact many looked ready to die, but at least they were not dangerous. When these people howled it was from physical pain, not psychic agony. Aside from the big cast on her arm, my mother's only problem was that she couldn't remember. Otherwise she was in perfect health. There was nothing wrong with her aside from fatal dementia, just like there had been nothing wrong with Jack but cancer. It only takes one thing to kill you.

After arranging the move with the doctor and administration, I arrived at Angel View after the orderlies had taken her few things and TV to the other side of the hospital, the "normal" section. When they had tried to take her there, though, she balked.

I said, "Let's just go look at the other room, OK?" The head nurse had to accompany us outside of the locked ward, and the three of us shuffled slowly down the hall. "Mom, see the pretty dining room, the piano, isn't it cheerful?"

"Oh no, it's too big. I'd get lost. Let's go back."

"Just wait till you see the new room. See the big pretty window?"

"No, I'd die if I had to stay here!" She was shaking all over with fear and nerves.

"Let's think about it," said the nurse, "maybe come back again later."

"No, no," shouted my mother.

I went to Central Library downtown for a librarians' meeting, my pockets stuffed with numbers of various agencies and facilities to call from the pay phone on my break. After two months, the cast was now off, and mom didn't need nursing, or to live in a nursing home. What she needed now was good board and care, not easy to find without a lot more income than Social Security.

I called Angel View and was relieved that Mom was no longer hysterical as she had been the night before when I visited after work. Jason had stayed overnight and succeeded in reassuring her. He had a calming way with her that I didn't have. These days I just made her mad.

———

Late that night Jason telephoned me and we argued. When I accused him of neglecting his responsibilities, for example, the rabbit ears for grandma's TV, he yelled, "What about Adam? Why isn't he here?" Just like when he was a kid. Jason was still a kid, I knew, despite being twenty-three years old. Jason then put me on call-waiting and I hung up. He didn't call back. I was under terrible stress, but then again so was he. All in all, I considered he was doing great under the circumstances.

I, too, wished Adam were here in L.A. Both Jason and I missed him. We all yearned for the family life we used to have, our comfortable home, and especially, we all missed Jack. They say a woman either marries her father or his opposite. I wouldn't say Jack was the opposite, because he and my father were both good men. But I remember as a teenager wishing for a father like Eric Sevareid, a famous war correspondent and award-winning CBS commentator. I remember him as dignified, wise and elegant, And he was of Norwegian heritage, just like Jack. Married to even-tempered Jack and seeing him come home every night on time, beautifully dressed in his made-to-order suits, dependable and there for anyone who needed him, I realized I had wanted a father like that. And how lucky I was to have such a man in my life at last.

Musical like his grandfather but hard-working and dedicated, Adam, a talented classical trombonist, who had never lost an audition or a scholarship as a teenager, who had attended the best music schools and conservatories in America on scholarship and had been the youngest orchestra member playing in the Spoletto Music Festival in Italy, gave up his promising musical career when he joined a strange, to me, sect in Northern California.

He moved to the mountains outside Sacramento to work on the commune as a laborer in the organization's prize-winning vineyard. Part of the cult's technique of keeping its educated and intelligent members was to woo them through the arts. And also, like most similar groups, to separate them from their families. So, even though I called and wrote frequently, I didn't expect him to visit Los Angeles often. I tried not to think of him up there living in a barn without heat or plumbing. But if I remembered the sweet and serious child he was or the teenager taking the RTD bus to L.A. Philharmonic concerts at the Music Center, or the young man playing his horn in orchestras under the batons of Daniel Lewis and Meli Mehta, I suffered too. I couldn't stand being completely out of his life. It wasn't supposed to be this way. I had no other family but my mother and sons, plus my aged but healthy and independent grandmother who lived in Palm Springs. Too bad she was a cactus on wheels.

I hated the blinking light on my answering machine. I could not bring myself to call back my mother's friends who left concerned messages wondering what had happened to her, and I was always afraid it was a nurse calling with bad news. I could not even call my grandmother (my father's mother) in Palm Springs. Being my mother's mother-in-law, she had a mean and jealous antipathy to her, so she seemed glad now that my mother was suffering, so I stopped talking about her. But at least my grandmother was in good health and independent and I didn't have to worry about her.

I did call Jason to plan the move to board and care. "You know I'm still paying for her old apartment. I haven't been able to face the fact that she can never live there again. That's all she talks about. Every day she says, 'You didn't give up my place, did you?' I can't deal with her furniture, clothes and stuff. Is there anything you want of hers?"

"I dunno...maybe...the rocking chair..."

"Go get it. I'm going to just call the Salvation Army to take it all. Her clothes don't fit anymore and she doesn't recognize any of her old stuff. When I took over some things of hers to the nursing home, she just got mad. 'Whose things are these?' she said. 'Where are my things?' I can't go through her stuff, it breaks my heart, the things she's saved, her little souvenirs. Nothing she has is worth anything except to her and now she doesn't recognize it. So please get what you want this week. I've been foolish to keep up my own hope and to humor her for these months by spending all the money to keep the apartment. It was never a realistic idea. So meet me at the nursing home Saturday? Grandma's not mad at you, it'll help her if you're there."

"Of course I'll be there. Don't worry."

I couldn't resist saying, "Well Jason, she hasn't seen

much of you lately!" and thinking sadly, that neither had I.

I arrived at the nursing home a few minutes after ten, happy to see Jason's blue jeep already in the parking lot. He was helping his grandmother put on her shoes and socks when I walked into the room. "Hi Mom. Are you ready to get out of here? You have done so well learning to do things with your left hand, and now that your cast is off, you can move to a better place, a quieter place."

"Oh yes, I want to get out of here. I don't know why you make me stay here, you're just terrible. We are going home, aren't we?"

"It's OK, Granny," Jason said. "Mom found a really nice new place to live." He was clipping the white enamel earrings she used to wear everyday onto her ears.

"Well I won't go. If I can't go home, I'll stay here." She was getting hysterical.

"Let's just go and see it," I said. "They're expecting us for lunch anyway. We'll just go for a nice ride and have lunch today. OK?"

"Is it far? I don't want to go far." Tears rolled down her cheeks.

A nurse came in with some water and a pill in a paper cup. I was glad I had requested a tranquilizer when I called the doctor. The doctor had seemed reluctant to sign my mother out, maybe because of the almost $3,000 per month they were getting from her Medicare and MediCal.

"No. What's this? I don't want it!" she pushed the nurse's arm away.

"It's just a vitamin pill to give you energy to have a nice day out," the nurse lied.

THE CHURCH OF TANGO

Jason put his arm around her. "Let's go, Granny."

The nurse punched in the secret door code, and the three of us shuffled slowly as one out the double doors and to my car. During the long ride out to Northridge on the freeway, my mother sat quietly crying in the passenger seat. She hadn't let Jason fasten the seat belt and that made me even more anxious.

We were met at the door of Sunny Acres Board and Care by Ruth, a well-dressed patient who carried a red purse. She smiled and bounced up and down as she grabbed Jason's arm. "Oh sweetie, I'm so glad to see you. It's been a long time. How is everybody at home? You were always my favorite, you know. Here, do you want to see my room?" And off they went down the hall, Jason looking back at me over his shoulder, shrugging good-naturedly.

The director, Alma, was there to meet us and I liked the way she looked carefully at my mother and spoke slowly and evenly. "Hi, Lee. So glad you could come today."

"Oh it was so far, so long to come. I don't really want to be here, you know. I want to go home."

I whispered that Mom had refused to bring her clothes, that she refused to move here from the nursing home and would only agree to move "home" to her old apartment in Hollywood. "I don't know what to do," I finished lamely.

The director continued to study my mother. "Lee, your daughter and grandson have to leave now. They have to go to work. They'll come back later." To me she said, "Go. It will be all right. She'll adjust. Go now."

"Just like that? What about her clothes?"

"We'll manage. You can bring them tomorrow."

I looked at Jason for guidance, but he looked torn to shreds. "OK, Jason? We have to go to work, right?"

Ruth sprang up and dragged Jason and me over to the bulletin board by the front door. "Want to see a picture of my mother?" pointing to a Polaroid of herself smiling in front of a birthday cake.

"OK, Mom," I took our proximity to the door as a sign. "We're going to work. We'll come back in a little while."

My mother forgot the ice cream she had been eating. "No, you can't leave me here. NO, NO!" She ran to the door, tears streaming down her terrified, angry face. "NO, NO!" she was screaming now. "I won't, I won't!" her tiny frail hands were fists helplessly beating the air.

I looked miserably at the director, who opened the locked front door and shooed us out. "She'll be all right. You can call me later." Then she shut and bolted the door.

Jason and I had a last look through the steel mesh screen door of our mother/grandmother, hysterical with rage. "I hate you, I hate you!" We could still hear her screams as we walked to the car, both of us in tears.

If God lived on earth, people would break his windows.

~ Jewish Proverb

CHAPTER 12

BAL MUSETTE

Love teaches even asses to dance.

~ French Proverb

I dug out an international calling card and telephoned Olivier from my office at the library. But first I practiced what I would say, to him and to his wife if she answered. When I got the answering machine, it flustered me and I hung up. An hour later I tried again and this time Olivier answered. "Where are you calling from?" he asked with surprise and pleasure in his deep voice.

"From work," I said.

"In the United States?"

"Yes, from the library. I want to wish you bon voyage. What will you do in Katmandu?" He had written to me about his vacation plans.

"Go trekking, take walks. When will you be in Paris?"

"Oh, I don't know, probably in May. Will you be too tired to see me from all those walks?"

"No," he laughed, "I'll be rested by then. Call me when you are here."

Throughout the brief conversation he sprinkled the French oral conjunction, "écoute... écoute," and I was listening, very hard. I could picture his face so easily as he talked, and imagined him using his arms in Gallic punctuation. The connection was excellent and effortless.

"Je t'embrasse," he said."A bientôt!"

I hung up, my heart pounding. It felt so good to talk to him, to hear his voice so close in my ear. Usually communicating in French on the telephone was difficult for me, but I understood Olivier perfectly.

I could tell he had changed towards me. He was warmer and more personal. What of his wife?

I was lucky that I could take more unpaid time off at work, thanks to a kind supervisor and my money box. After what happened to Jack I didn't want to put off any pleasure. Who knew he would die so young? We couldn't afford it at the time, but I was so thankful we had taken nice vacations and went to great restaurants and threw terrific parties, because if not, he never would have experienced those pleasures. Why wait for a "someday" that may never come?

Before leaving again for France at the end of May, I went out to the Valley to visit my mother and her caretakers. She had forgotten her anger at being moved to the board and care facility, and had settled in as though Sunny Acres had always been home, which in fact for her it had, as she could no longer recollect anyplace else. I took her out to a coffee shop. Mom couldn't remember that she used to love coffee as much as I, and let it grow cold in the cup. In fact, she no longer remembered me.

But later, when Alma put on some Glen Miller music, my mother remembered how to dance.

In his little Renault, Olivier and I chugged to Giverny and Monet's gardens, an hour's drive from Paris. The weather was perfect; the water lilies, irises, and wisteria (the same purple as the jacaranda trees in L.A.) bloomed under the warm sun, and I walked on flower-scented air, hand in hand with Olivier as if in a dream. We took pictures of each other on the bridge, by Monet's little boat in the lake, under the weeping willow, in Monet's jonquil-yellow kitchen. Monet! And just a few hours ago I was in Los Angeles.

The next day I went to Olivier's apartment for lunch. His seventeenth-century building in the Marais had no elevator, and I walked up five flights of worn varnished wood stairs. He was in the kitchen when I arrived, wearing an apron, sautéing and stirring something that smelled of garlic and rosemary. The table was set with damask linens, large heavy European silver flatware placed upside-down (to me) beside the old, cracked porcelain dinner plates.

Olivier's apartment was not at all what I had expected. Far from the little artist's studio I had envisioned when I mooned over him last year in French class, it was in fact huge, especially for Paris: five large rooms with four fireplaces, ancient red tile floors, a modern washer in the roomy bathroom, an antique stove in the kitchen, computer on his heirloom desk, Asian artifacts mixed with modern art and oriental rugs, American jazz (Ella) on the stereo, a black cat. The whole effect was like that of a movie set, or a dream. I wondered how much of the décor his wife had done, and I chose to overlook the bottles of perfumes and framed photographs.

After the simple meal, he took me to see two more Parisian gardens. It was spring, Paris was in fragrant flower, and I was over-dosing on sensuality. The song *April in Paris* was not written for nothing.

Perhaps it's true wherever there are four seasons, that in spring the sap moves in the trees, and the blood moves in the people. In Paris that afternoon in May at the Château de Vincennes, people of all ages were dancing frenetically to a loud samba band. Packed into a tent, they were out of control, under the dominion of music and springtime. I guess I went out of control myself. When Olivier and I were resting in each other's arms on the grass in the Parc de Fleurs I blurted out in French, "You know that I love you, Olivier, je brulais d'amour, that I've burned with love for you since we met fifteen months ago!"

In response he kissed me, a kiss without time.

Olivier was expressive and expansive and filled the air with his words. I was hypnotized beyond reason by his voice. As for my French, things I knew very well escaped me entirely. I threw together verbs and nouns and bad pronunciation and he probably didn't know what I was saying at all. I told him I loved him. He understood that. It felt good to say it, I guess that's why people do. Of course he said nothing, I knew he wouldn't.

When Oliver took me to the bedroom that first evening and switched on the light, several small lamps came on at once illuminating the large wooden art nouveau bed in one corner, surrounded by built-in wooden floor-to-ceiling bookcases filled with what looked to me like every book ever written in every language on Tibet. There was an ornate fireplace with an old mantel on which sat a bowl of fresh hydrangeas reflected in a cracked gilded mirror. The two large French windows giving onto the street were covered by red draperies that would in the morning cast a rosy glow on our bare white bodies in the bed under real linen sheets hand-embroidered with lace.

Olivier had the most beautiful body I had ever seen, hairless but for thick black curls on his head and around his genitals. How could it be that a man who was almost fifty had such white perfect skin without a blemish on it? To be still so naturally strong and muscular? I had never seen an uncircumcised man before, and his groin looked to me like Italian sculpture, with a penis the loveliest color of rose. By the lamplight, he looked deep into my eyes the whole time he made love to me, seeing, I imagined, my soul.

He slept silently and peacefully beside me that night. I didn't sleep at all. The trains of the Métro rumbled through vast tunnels far below, making the bed vibrate like small earthquakes far away in Los Angeles, or maybe it was my excitement. Once in a while in the dark, the small black cat, Minette, padded across my stomach.

We slept late on Sunday. And we stayed in bed even later. We finally got up and into the shower, but when I soaped him up and made him hard, he dragged me out of the bathroom, all wet and soapy myself, and back into the bed. He wore his reading glasses when we made love. What could be more flattering to me than that?

The morning had almost vanished when we found ourselves facing each other over the kitchen table having breakfast. "We must hurry," he said, "the market closes soon and we have nothing for dinner." In France, unlike L.A. where you could buy food or television sets at all hours of the day and night, seven days a week, here people had to plan ahead. There were strict laws about what shops could be open when, and Sunday afternoon everything was closed. If you had nothing to eat at home on Sunday you went hungry or to a restaurant.

To get to the market—I thought we were going to a supermarket, like Safeway—we walked through quiet Sunday-sleepy neighborhoods with no signs of life, him pulling the shopping cart with one hand and holding tight to me with the other. Suddenly there appeared an ornamental arch of verdigris cast iron heralding the bustling little market street of Rue Montorgueil. For pedestrians only this morning, the gray marble cobblestoned street had the ambiance and gaiety of a village fair.

At Le Paradis des Fruits he bought a box of tiny fraises des bois. On to Aux Fins Herbages Normands for delicate lamb chops, Le Temple du Fromage (owned by a defrocked priest, Olivier explained) for cheese. At the blue-tiled fishmonger's, Aux Ecailles d'Argent, the staff, in rubber aprons and high rubber boots, served their customers amidst the displays of magnificent whole fish posed on seas of ice. We looked in the window of La Fontaine au Chocolat to see a fountain of flowing chocolate surrounded by chocolate sculptures of butterflies and ladies' high-heeled slippers. All these—to me— exotic delicacies with French names in shops that were more interesting than any museum. Exquisite, glorious food!

When the shopping cart was full, he asked if I wanted a coffee at the café in the middle of the street. I flashed him a grateful smile as I realized that was just what I wanted. We got the last little table on the cobblestones, and sat there side-by-side, like at the theater, with tiny cups of espresso.

We watched the street life as if it were a play: the young mothers with strollers, the old ladies with little dogs, the teenagers in smoky packs, the beggars, the elegant women with long black-stockinged legs, the old men with their cigars, an accordion player—all the movie clichés were real. Off to the right was a display of stacked boxes of fruit juice and a noisy vendor who, like a carnival barker, loudly and comically tried to convince shoppers of the incredible bargain he offered. I wouldn't have been at all surprised if he had launched the boxes of juice high into the air and juggled them. Olivier and I looked at each other and laughed.

———

"La Bibliothèque Nationale, et VITE!' If I had known how to say "and step on it!" in French, I would have. The driver understood my anxiety, especially when I told him there was romance involved and I was to meet a man who had waited for me too long the last time. We seemed to fly across Paris, cutting through the traffic like a hot knife in ripe Camembert, arriving in fifteen minutes. Olivier was there, leaning against the high stone wall of the library. I said, "Le voilà!" and threw a fifty-franc note to the driver over the back of the seat and dashed across the street, heedless of the cars.

Olivier and I embraced and kissed while the taxi driver watched; I could hear the motor idling. Finally we broke apart and I sneaked a look at the driver, who waved and smiled as he drove off, content, I supposed being French, that he had helped along the course of love that day.

Later over coffee we talked about the exhibit we had just seen—Le Printemps de Génie—at the National Library. And then he invited me to the Titian exhibit at the Grand Palais on the Champs D'Elysee. It was wonderful to be with a man who knew and cared about art, and of course, to see so much of it in Paris. But I was troubled about becoming too comfortable, too happy.

"Olivier, maybe not. Maybe we just shouldn't go any farther. I am getting a little afraid of my feelings." I thought I might be up for an affair with someone, but not for falling in love with a married man. I needed some pleasure and fun, but not more pain and heartbreak. My feelings for Olivier were already running deep.

"Bien, if you do not care to go…I understand. Perhaps it is better."

So we left it like that.

I wanted privacy from curious Madame who always eavesdropped on every call her roomers made, and so a few days later I phoned Olivier from the Métro. I had been agonizing about what to do, whether to proceed, and couldn't sleep until I made a decision. It was so noisy I couldn't hear or understand him at first. I said I would very much like to go to the Titian exhibit if he still wanted to. I had refused his invitation out of fear of being hurt, that this situation was too hot for me to handle. I never wanted to love a married man.

———

Olivier was waiting for me at the Grand Palais, reading at the top of the elegant staircase. I could see him from a distance as I walked from the Métro. I felt like the setting sun shone only on me. I wanted time to stop, the anticipation so intensely delicious that I wanted to freeze the moment and just enjoy it as long as possible, revel in it, luxuriate in it. Like that exquisite instant when you're making love and you know you are going to come.

He seemed hesitant, almost shy. When I hugged him and kissed him as before and looked into his eyes and smiled, he said, "J'étais heureux que tu m'as appelée," I am happy you called me. (thinking about it later I figured it wasn't exactly that, it would have had to be in the subjunctive.)

Afterwards, we went to Café Beaubourg in Les Halles. Looking down at my kir, I asked him, "Are you angry, do you forgive me, for saying I couldn't see you anymore?"

He said he couldn't understand why I had been afraid. I told him one reason that I was afraid was because I loved his apartment so much. (I didn't say I could see his wife in it everywhere, or that I could see myself living there with him.) When he told me he had designed and decorated it himself over a period of sixteen years, I admired him even more.

So now at the café I tried to explain a little. "Since I came to Paris wanting to see you, it does seem stupid not to make the most of these two weeks."

He replied that after all, I did know he was married.

"Yes," I said quietly, looking down at my hands folded in my lap, "but by the time I found out it was already too late."

"Tu sais, Cherie, I have not been happy for many years."

"Why not?"

"We just drifted into getting married in the first place. We were living together and Delfine wanted legal property rights, although the apartment was a gift to me from my father long before we married."

"Were you in love? Did you ever think of separating?"

"I do not think we ever really loved each other, it was just convenient to be married. I never felt the way I feel about you. Now I have decided I want to divorce. I want my freedom and obviously she wants hers too, because she is always away from France. If she contests, and she will certainly as she wants the property, a divorce can take seven years.

"Seven years? I don't believe it!" I said.

"And I could lose everything if the judge has sympathy for her. It is very complicated in France. And it means my friends must write testimonies about the marriage; who is right, who is wrong. But I will take the risk."

He kissed me a lot right there in the café, then. I didn't know what it meant to kiss so much in public. Was it him or just very French?

That night I slept with him, only slept because I began my period. I kept my panties on. I dreamed I was on a boat on the sea, and I knew a strong wave was going to swamp the deck so I braced myself for it. When it came, it hit me with such cold violence, it woke me up. Then I lay there, frightened and anxious, on my back with my eyes open in the dark, feeling Olivier sleep quietly next to me as the trains rumbled toward their destinies in the dark passageways far below.

CHAPTER 13

LA VIE EN ROSE

*If you don't know where you're going, you'll end up
somewhere else.*

~ Yogi Berra

Paris in springtime is a garden. Window boxes, squares, parks, gardens, shops and people flaunt bright blossoms everywhere. Paris was in flower and so was I. It seemed like tout Paris knew I was in love. Wherever I went during these days, whatever I did, men paid me attention in ways that made me feel beautiful, young and desirable. And the more that happened, the more I bloomed, a flower in the sun under the cloudy Paris skies. The French even had a special word for what was happening to me, *épanouir*.

Olivier continued to show me his Paris, and I felt so special that it would soon be mine too. We went to concerts of early baroque music in the stained-glass splendor of Sainte Chappelle, and of nineteenth-century funeral music in the subterranean Catacombs. Another evening we went to a gypsy circus on a tiny side street near the Place de Clichy. After we watched the gypsies put the animals to bed by the light of a blazing bonfire, we went to Au Pied du Cochon in Les Halles for onion soup, and sat with the night workers, tourists and famous film stars until two in the morning.

On Saturday when the phone rang at Madame's, I knew it was Olivier. He called to ask me to stay with him for my last few days in Paris. He would come around for me in his car in an hour. I was stunned.

I wrote a check for the full amount to Madame, and told her I was in love. Madame was ecstatic, delighted to hear of this new development in the American widow's life.

Chez Olivier, he watched my pleasure at listening to his Baroque opera with satisfaction as he did the dishes. Between arias he commented on the early instruments, voices, and plot, and at one point danced in front of me in his damp and soiled apron, rolling his eyes heavenward and gesturing theatrically with a wooden spoon.

I didn't know how to be taken care of. All of my life it had been me who had done the caretaking—my children, my sick husband, my mother. I tried to remember when last someone made me feel pampered and cherished like this and couldn't. I didn't remember ever the normal feeling children can have of security and absolute certainty their parents will take the best care of them possible. I didn't remember being able to relax and luxuriate in the comforts of not being ready to deal with disaster. There was always a disaster in my parents' lives that caused them to fall apart, and I knew I had better not count on them. I knew from toddlerhood I had to count on myself, but also it was plain to me I needed to worry about them as well. As an only child I was always allowed to have pets—from red eared turtles with designs painted on their shells from Olvera Street, to tropical fish, to cats and dogs. But every single pet had a bad end. I worried about them constantly, but I couldn't prevent my parents from letting the puppies run freely outside or force them to get the animals inoculated and cared for by a vet when they were sick. My pets, along with my parents, were additional worries for my child self. So I grew up always on guard and self-reliant. Now there was someone physically caring for me and it felt wonderful.

In the bathroom I tried to be careful not to disturb anything. I was frightened of touching or even seeing anything belonging to his wife, so I averted my eyes from the half-empty bottles of makeup and cosmetics. His apartment held so many clues to his nature, it was like a treasure chest waiting to be opened, but I couldn't even touch a book on the shelf. I looked at all the titles with my hands clasped behind my back, like I used to direct my children to do in shops. I was perfectly content to know what he wished me to know. Maybe I was afraid to know too much, to find out something that might make me uncomfortable.

Because he was lonely and unhappy and it seemed to me that Delfine, his wife, certainly didn't care about him or she would stay home from Katmandu, I felt no guilt or remorse to be in love with a married man. There were no children as neither had wanted them, no home and hearth, no lying or sneaking. It seemed to me that this stagnant marriage had been over for a very long time, and that both Olivier and Delfine could only improve their lives by separating and moving on. It wasn't right that this man was living without love and affection. How could his wife abandon him like that?

The next morning, the day of my departure, we sat at the little kitchen table, hugging our bowls of tea, staring miserably into each other's eyes. I was conscious of trying not to look droopy, sad and depressed. I wanted him to remember my smile. My hands were trembling so that I could hardly hold my bowl and the tartine wouldn't go down my throat. At last I pushed him towards the door. "Vas-y! Au bulot! You have students waiting," I said. I said it so low and badly that he thought I said au revoir and he said the dreaded words, the ones I never wanted to hear from him, back to me. And then he was gone.

I realized that when two people's spirits are close and love each other, it is easier to separate physically because they are emotionally and psychologically connected. If there were only physical intimacy, then the detached, lonely feelings take precedence when the bodies part.

I needed to proceed on the basis that these few days might be all there ever was. He may or may not get divorced. He may or may not want me, love me in the future. I couldn't build my life on the fantasy of being with him. I couldn't drop everything to move to Paris to do nothing, after all. When you're young and in love you think in terms of a family, building a career, someday buying a house. What did you plan with someone when you're pushing fifty? Doesn't a person need meaningful work, a separate life of goals and accomplishments, even if they're small? Or was being together enough?

Was I completely crazy to think of opening a dance club in a foreign land, gambling all of my nest egg?

French cowboy dance clubs, import-export of garden snails, a job in a French library—whatever it took.

In Evian, I was welcomed cordially at Chez Danic and shown to a shady table looking out at the lake under the arbor of fragrant pink and red cabbage roses. I noticed another woman eating alone at the other end of the garden, sitting there with her gray hair and glass of red wine. There was a man lunching by himself too, but for company he had a stack of books and magazines. As I sat under the rose arbor in a garden by the side of the road, looking at the sun shining on Switzerland across the blue-green water, I was happy.

Businessmen in suits had motored over from Lausanne in little speedboats on their lunch hour and docked next to the arbor. They lounged with loosened neckties around the white plastic tables covered in pink cloths, admiring their home city across the lake in another land, puffing contentedly on cigars. A graceful slim woman in immaculate yellow linen ran back and forth across the busy road between the restaurant and rose arbor, dodging traffic in her high heeled mules, carrying orders to the kitchen and drinks to us on a tray. Here, as everywhere in the village each spring, wafted the heavy sweet perfume of cherry jam boiling in kitchens for miles around, combining with the scent of the drowsy roses, and intoxicating the air.

I had not eaten there in the garden since three years ago exactly, one year before Jack's death. The best Thanksgiving dinner we ever had was there the November we came together with co-owners Sam and Susie to furnish the new apartment. The staff had been unsure of exactly how to prepare the traditional turkey and trimmings we ordered and so had given the dishes an unforgettable French flair: the cranberry sauce was a light glaze poured over the spit-roasted golden bird, the pumpkin pie flavored with lemon. We were served in the cozy winter dining room by the open fire, our table decorated with tiny American flags.

Now I recognized the elegant owner, and the maitre d' who took my order, but the young waitresses in their long black skirts and white ruffled aprons were all new to me. I loved hearing the crunch on the gravel of their polished black shoes as they bustled to serve their fortunate customers.

I chose a multi-course menu, a kir, a glass of local red wine, a half bottle of Evian. And then I leaned back in my padded garden chair and prepared to be taken care of. When the aperitif arrived along with pretty little hors d'oeuvres, I raised my glass. Here's to you, Jack.

Three people wished me "Bon appétit" as I began a meal of Parma ham and melon, followed by a hot goat cheese salad. The waitress touched the handles of my knife and fork three different times to make sure they were positioned properly. The sun shone on me and the roses and cherries scented the air and swans glided by a few feet from my table.

The meal of many things included tiny lobster tails and a small, three-chop rack of lamb cooked over a wood fire there in the garden. During the dessert course (I had two!) it started to rain. I felt dry and snug and pampered under the large umbrella as I watched the staff scurry around to bring in the cushions and linens. None of the diners made any effort to hasten and leave because of the change in the weather, even the Swiss businessmen continued to enjoy their relaxed conversation over their espressos. The lone man across from me carried on reading and sipping his coffee, as oblivious to the rain as he had been to the sun. When it rains in Los Angeles, it's cold, but here the air was warm and perfect. Everything was perfect.

In the afternoon I hiked up to the cemetery to lay some roses on Jack's grave. People who didn't know me well couldn't believe or understand why the boys and I flew to France with the square copper box of his ashes under my airplane seat. "Why are you doing such a strange thing? Was that what Jack wanted? Was he French? Won't your sons be upset?" Jack never said he cared one way or another about his final resting place, but I knew he would be delighted. Maybe he was delighted. He used to love to go around saying in his impossible, almost non-existent French, "Je suis natif!" And now he was a native. The puzzled village priest had tried to comprehend an American woman in his study requesting a burial service, but he agreed to do it. He didn't even ask why, or if Jack had been Catholic.

It was a hot morning in October eighteen months before when the tombstone company delivered a polished gray granite headstone to the tiny cemetery behind the church of Lugrin. There was his name in bronze letters, *Jack G. Magnus, 1937-1991, cher époux et papa*, and a simple cross. In the country cemeteries in France flowers were planted directly on the graves, and that day the cemetery was abloom with gold, purple and bronze chrysanthemums, as was the custom for the approaching festival of Toussaint, All Saints' Day.

While the three workmen completed the digging, I looked down to the lake and saw the swans Jack had loved so much. If I turned around I would see the local mountains directly behind, the Memises of the French Alps. The different toned bells on the cows that grazed the fields around the cemetery chimed in harmony. The young workman handled the copper box with reverence and care, placing it deeply in the opening. The earth matched the color of the box as it sat there, small and alone, so unlike Jack in life. I threw a handful of the copper-colored dirt into the grave and one by one so did the boys and the small gathering of French friends.

Everyone has to die, some sooner rather than later. I accepted that. Some deaths are better than others, though, and I couldn't accept that not only did Jack have to die too young and in terrible pain, but he had a "bad death." He was in the Home Hospice program at Kaiser Hospital, but on Saturday night I had to call an ambulance because of sudden, horrible pain that couldn't be eased. Saturday night is not a good time to go to the ER in Hollywood; the waiting room was packed with gunshot wounds and bleeders. There were no beds, so he lay on a gurney in the hall for the longest time. I had to scream like Shirley MacLaine in *Terms of Endearment* to get a doctor's attention. He glanced at Jack's chart and knew he was going to die, so lost interest. Jack was put back into an ambulance and taken across the street to the hospice, and given a room shared with a Mexican man.

The next day was Sunday and Fathers' Day. Jack's bed was by the door and all day long streams of people filed past to visit the other man in the bed by the window, bringing balloons, presents, food, and ranchero music on a boombox. Little girls in pink party dresses, babies, and revelers were in and out all day as I sat with my dying husband, who was still, despite the morphine drip, in immense pain. I grabbed the doctor. "Please can't you make him comfortable at least?"

"I'm sorry. We can't give him any more morphine."

"Because you're afraid it will kill him? He's dying!"

The doctor looked uneasy. "But we can't kill him. I'm sorry he has to suffer." And he left the room of death and merrymakers.

The chaplain came in and asked to speak to me in the hall. I didn't want to leave Jack, but the chaplain said it would only take a moment. Outside the room, he told me Jack was going to die soon, and asked if I was prepared. Meanwhile, when I left, Jack did too. I guess he didn't want me to watch, so he waited. But I wanted to be there. I was there during this entire nightmare journey, but I missed the ending. I didn't want him to go alone.

One of the party-goers passed by then on his way out and stopped to say, "I'm sorry about your father." The suffering and disease had aged his body thirty years.

———

Now, two years later, the afternoon showers that began during my Chez Danic lunch that afternoon turned into a storm brewing over the lake. I reached my apartment just in time. The water below my balcony was dark, mysterious, full of power; the restless sky all colors of gray, pierced by occasional stabs of lightening. Next door, Michel was on his balcony with his field glasses, listening to the CB radio in case he had to go rescue a boat in the volunteer-fireman way of small villages. Floriane was exultant and animated, Edith looked exhausted.

Contemplating the lake and the mountains and the heavens outside my windows, I danced before the fire to the music of the thundering storm.

CHAPTER 14

GALA FINALE

If you want a happy ending, that depends, of course,
on where you stop your story.

~ Orson Welles

I knew for sure I wasn't in France anymore when someone let a door swing back in my face, almost hitting me. The gallant riders of the Paris Métro took pride in not doing that. The buses did not display posters of poetry and people did not excuse themselves when they bumped into you in crowds. The graffiti was not the Je t'aime written on the base of the lion statue in the Place Denfert, but Fuck you! I was back in Los Angeles.

It had been almost a month since I had heard from Olivier, since I left Paris to return to L.A.. Had he changed his mind about me and/or the divorce? Had he fallen back in love with his wife during her return to Paris? Was he sick? Should I write again, call or do nothing? Every day when I opened my mailbox and there was no letter from him, I was crushed. It all seemed like a dream—that Olivier existed, let alone that he loved me. After all, he was Paris to me; was I America to him?

The longing was physical. The yearning to be in France, that old-fashioned country-song feeling, was so strong. It was as if my soul were out of my body, stretching itself thin in an arc towards Europe, leaving only a mist of ectoplasm functioning in L. A.

There is a moment, a split-second, when, as you curve around on Figueroa Street and cross onto Riverside Drive going north as I did every night after work, that the Los Angeles River could be the Seine. Every time I caught that glimpse out of the corner of my eye, especially at night and in the rare California rain, I was transported with desire to be back in Paris. But it wasn't the Seine, it was a concrete-lined storm channel, and I was in L.A. 6,000 miles away.

I did something I was ashamed of: I called Olivier and when he answered, hung up. I had debated doing it for days, the pros and cons of what might happen and how I would feel. I pictured my call moving through amber fields and over purple mountains and under shining seas to the beaches of St. Tropez, up the river to Paris, and snaking through old cobblestone streets.

"Allô?" he said.

I heard his voice. We were connected for two seconds. We were united, together across six thousand miles for the length of a breath. During a heartbeat we were joined. And I knew then that he was all right. Only those not in love take the telephone for granted.

The next day his letter arrived, reiterating his love for me, his need for me in his life, and how he hoped one day to divorce. "I never before knew true love and happiness," he wrote. "Come to me soon!"

But he also wrote how divorce can take up to seven years in France, and he must keep our affair from his wife, who would be given everything if adultery were proven against him. There was no such thing as no-fault divorce in France. Guilt must be established. "Mais viens, ma chérie," he wrote, "tout se passera bien".

At last I was going to my lover—Paris. And if love were a sin, then I was going to hell.

Now that I knew I was leaving, my Park La Brea apartment didn't seem so bad. Every night when I came home from work I was greeted by the elegant view of the city lights behind the splendor of the Knabe grand piano standing on the maroon and blue Kashan rug. Outside my tower windows were long rows of tall palm trees. When the Western sun shone on the dead brown fronds turning them into gold, and illuminated the tips of the green fans on the treetops, they seemed to be set on fire, the ends burning from the glistening sun. A nightly sunset miracle, why didn't I ever notice before how beautiful it was?

For the first time in my life I would be without an address. When the movers came to take my things to storage and the apartment was no longer mine, my twenty-five year library career would be over, and I would stand alone on the sidewalk with a suitcase in each hand, just like I did in what seemed a lifetime ago, that Sunday morning in Paris. For the first time in my life I would own no keys: no house key, no car key, no work key. But as the old saying goes, as one door closes, another opens. And I was dancing across the new threshold.

CHAPTER 15

CANCER DANCER

The fight is won or lost far away from witnesses - behind the lines, in the gym and out there on the road, long before I dance under those lights.

~ Muhammad Ali

That's what should have happened, that's the happy ending I wanted. Yet after the door shut on my L.A. life, I entered once again through the portals of cancer, only this time it was me.

During my final routine physical exam before the move to Paris, the jovial doctor's round face had fallen in the middle of a joke about France. His fingers worriedly palpated the soft side of my right breast. "How long have you had this lump?" he asked, suddenly all merriment gone.

Scared, but not too scared because I had had exams and regular mammograms since Jack died, I said, "Oh I don't know, a couple of years. I had a mamo three or four months ago and nobody said anything. Besides, according to what I've read, I have zero risk factors for breast cancer." No one in my family had it, I breast fed my babies, had no breast "issues" like dense tissue or benign lumps, wasn't overweight, and exercised, all of the "healthy breast stuff."

He was already on the phone. "OK, I'll send her down

immediately. All right, young lady," he said turning to me, "You're to go downstairs and have a biopsy. The surgeon will do it on his lunch hour so we can get this thing figured out and you can run off to France." He smiled, but there was no humor in it.

The procedure didn't take long, nor did it hurt. Soon I was putting on my blouse and buttoning it up over the large bandage on my chest. "So now what, Doc?" I asked.

"We wait for the lab results. And hope it's nothing."

So I went back to work, and I waited. I stopped packing and planning. I only waited. A week later I got a call when I was working the reference desk at the busiest time, right after school, and the library was full of patrons.

"Reference. May I help you?" I answered the phone.

"Mrs. Magnus? This is Dr. Solomon. I'm sorry to say that your test came back positive."

"Positive?" I repeated, looking around the busy reading room in panic and the group of teenagers congregated around the desk where I sat. "What does that mean?"

"It means a malignancy. Please make an appointment to come in and see me. We have to discuss what we're going to do."

"I have cancer? But I can't, I'm moving to France. My husband had cancer, not me." All of a sudden the busy bustling library was completely silent, all of the patrons still, only the word "cancer" echoed loudly around the room.

I put the receiver down on the reference desk, and went upstairs to the open mezzanine that was the library workroom. I didn't know what to do, so I stood there. I guessed I should go home, call people for support, but who? My mother couldn't understand, nor did I want her to. My sons. My grandmother? Olivier. What I really wanted to do was smash crockery and china dishes and pottery, to throw plates and vases against rocks the size of mountains, to hurl and pitch Carnival Glass and Fiestaware and pate de verre and crystal ashtrays and saucers won at fairs with tossed dimes, until there was a quarry of shards higher than my apartment at Park La Brea. But I stood silently in the workroom until I could gather up my purse, find a librarian to take over the reference desk, and go home.

I called Olivier first (his wife had gone back to Nepal.) "Oh please come, please be here for my surgery." For I knew before the doctor told me that the cancer had to be cut out.

Then I called Adam, who, from the middle of his cult compound where he was working in the fields for the guru, cried aloud at the news.

When Jason heard I was sick, his reply was that I was always sick. So then I told him how sick, and he went into immediate denial.

Olivier took a leave from the French school, which was glad to save some salary as the school was floundering, and came to Los Angeles the night before my surgery. I was happy to buy his ticket.

I had a lumpectomy and a lymphnodectomy, which wasn't too bad in the scheme of things. It wasn't like having a kidney removed or open-heart surgery. The night I came home from the hospital, Olivier and I made love, even with my attached drain and abundant bandages and anesthesia headache. He measured the fluid in the drain every few hours, and changed my bandages. I was happy.

We went out to Sunny Acres to see my mom, and Olivier

charmed her. She thought he was Maurice Chevalier, and he humored her and broke out in "Thank Heaven for Little Girls," and kissed her hand. With the drain and tubing covered by a long sweatshirt, we went to the Santa Monica Beach for a celebration of the 50th anniversary of D-Day. The French navy was there, a military band played *La Marseilleise,* lots of French and American mingling. When we returned to my apartment in Park La Brea, he asked me to marry him. "In France, divorces can take seven years! Will you be patient?"

I nodded. Of course I would be patient. I had work of my own to do—to get well.

Then he returned to Paris, and I began chemotherapy. I was petrified with fear and couldn't sleep the night before my first chemo. I had read all I could about the drugs Adriamycin and Cytoxin which I would be getting, and I knew how lethal they were. If a drop of the cherry red Adria spilled on your skin, you were burned. I just hoped it would be lethal to the cancer in my body.

People like to say, I said it too, "Oh no, I would never have chemo!" But when the doctor tells you it's do or die, you do it. I didn't think once about not doing it.

The two and a half hours of the IV drip passed uneventfully; no Adria was spilled and I didn't vomit. When Nancy took me home to Park La Brea and asked how else she could help, I didn't have an answer. I didn't want food, or drink, or conversation. She dropped me off, and I took the elevator upstairs to the thirteenth floor.

It was summer, and my penthouse with the western afternoon sun beating through the panoramic windows was unbearably hot. I would have liked to sit outside on a balcony or terrace, but there was none. I didn't know what to do, I didn't want to do anything.

A few days later Nancy took me shopping for head coverings at St John's hospital in Santa Monica where they had a "cancer boutique." My hair had not yet started falling out, but the doctor assured me that it would. Nancy enthused over various cotton turbans and scarves, and I bought all she liked, plus a couple of washable cotton hats with fabric flowers jauntily pinned to the brims. I thought I should look at wigs, too, but somehow the idea seemed just too hot. I was really suffering now with the heat. The surgery and the drugs thrust me immediately into "chemo pause," and the hot flashes came every ten minutes, day and night. There was no escape from the crushing heat. Most of the time I just lay on my bed and sweated. When a hot flash struck, it was like standing on hot coals in the flames of hell. It felt like my brain was on fire.

Several of my co-workers and friends brought over food and shared their company because eating was becoming almost impossible. Everything tasted off or bad, I had no strength or interest to plan and cook a meal for myself, and anyway, I felt full all of the time. It meant a lot to me that folks I wasn't even that close to, took the time and trouble to care that I ate.

My hair started falling out as predicted, three weeks to the day of my first chemo. Nancy had taken me on a picnic to Malibu, and when I reached up to scratch my head, hanks of hair came out with my hand. When I got home I immediately called Jason. "Come over quick and bring your hair clippers!"

He stood me in the bathtub and shaved my head. He swept it all up and threw it away in the bottom of the trash, while I studied my naked head from all sides with a hand mirror. "Mom, you have a beautiful head. Bald isn't a bad look on you!" We both laughed, and then I cried. I was glad to get this part over with all at once, and not have the little deaths of hair on my pillow and filling up the drain. At least it was cooler with no hair.

I hated wigs, but wearing cotton scarves wasn't too terrible, although the first thing I did coming home when I closed the front door behind me was to rip off whatever was covering my head. Somehow it gave me claustrophobia. If someone unexpectedly rang the doorbell, I always warned them before opening the door: "Watch out! I'm not wearing anything on my head!"

Without hair I didn't have to worry about waxing or shaving. I looked so strange without eyebrows or eyelashes. Even with big earrings I didn't feel very feminine. Without her "crowning glory," a woman loses so much of her power, like Sampson. When men go bald it's normal and acceptable, not a sign of catastrophic illness and possible death that frightens many people away from hairless women.

I was born an extra-sensitive person. I could hear, smell, feel things that others were oblivious to. Most of the time it was wonderful as I could enjoy and feel an ecstatic emotional experience to the hilt, but sometimes it made me suffer—when the music was too loud in jazz clubs, when food or drink didn't taste just right, when lights were too bright, when perfume was too strong. I had an extremely sensitive "startle" reflex. Fireworks were off-limits, as well as patriotic cannon firings. I got dizzy and nauseous in large stores and supermarkets where so much merchandise clamored for my attention, and I got seasick in revolving restaurants. I was the princess who couldn't sleep on a stack of mattresses because there was a pea underneath the bottom one. I loved suspense movies but often watched them from behind my hands. My sensitivities made me allergic to many substances, especially smoke of any kind and chemical odors. When I was a child I missed more school than I attended because I was always sick with a "cold." Now I knew it was a reaction to my father's chain smoking.

Other patients on the same chemo were not so strongly affected by side effects. I liked to think that my sensitivity made the drugs more lethal to the cancer cells in my body.

The drugs did something to my nerves, and I couldn't bear noise of any kind. I couldn't listen to music, play the piano, or leave the windows open for air, as the metal vertical blinds clacked together and made me crazy. It was as if all my nerve endings had been sandpapered. I couldn't read either, as I lost all powers of concentration. I couldn't think. The one thing I could do, and did do, was watch French movies on video. On a good day I would watch two. If I was able, I drove to Rocket Video on La Brea every day. I kept a notebook with the names and directors so I could remember which I had seen and tell Olivier about them.

I had a file of papers from my oncologist, psychologist, and radiologist stating in detail that my memory was affected by the chemo, as well as my concentration, my physical abilities and my nervous mental state. And that I was not able to work. As a librarian, I needed all of those faculties to do my job. Since I had no extended sick leave or any other income, I went to the Social Security office with the file to apply for Disabled Widow's Benefits under Jack's Social Security, which he didn't live long enough to collect. I was told that "it" was decided that I could indeed work, despite the doctors' statements to the contrary, and I was denied. But I couldn't work—I couldn't even read. I was so thankful to have some funds to lean on.

Olivier telephoned me every morning exactly at nine a.m. I awoke early and would just stare at the phone, waiting for his call. Afterwards, I was blue because I knew I would have to wait another twenty-four hours to talk to him again. We didn't have much to talk about; what the doctor said, what movies I saw, what his lawyer said, what his friends had written in their "testimonies" about the marriage, how his divorce was going, or not going. Sometimes he was fuming about particulars in his divorce proceedings and he would read to me from one paper or another and I could hear him angrily shuffling and flipping papers even after the topic changed to something else.

Because of Olivier's proposal of marriage once he had his divorce, now as a distraction I shopped for a wedding dress when I was up to it. I found a simple ivory dress at Macy's, and drove to a hat shop in Beverly Hills one hot morning and bought a wispy headpiece in the same color. (I had to try it on over my wig.) I picked up some ivory lace pumps in the shoe store on Hollywood Boulevard next to the wig shop.

I had a wild idea: why not go to Paris to be with Olivier? If I could have a chemotherapy treatment there, I could be with him for five weeks if my doctor said okay. Dr. Hadassian, my oncologist, thought it would be a great idea to get all those endorphins from love and making love, and so gave his permission. Olivier found an oncologist in Paris who agreed to give me the treatment at the Hôpital Saint-Louis with the same drugs I was taking in L.A.

Yes, sure, I was being extravagant, impetuous and spontaneous. Perhaps I was that way because of my dad. While he didn't live long enough for us to mend our fences over his drinking and smoking, my best childhood memories were of his extravagant and spontaneous acts with me. One of my earliest recollections was sitting in his lap at three years of age, facing the sun in his open cockpit airplane, flying up and up to the heavens without a parachute, my mother on the ground worried sick.

Ten years later one Saturday morning I mentioned that my dancing idol, Donald O'Connor, was appearing at the Sahara Hotel in Las Vegas, and my father said, "Let's go!" The three of us piled into the Mercury and drove to Vegas, my dad somehow scoring a table right down front for the show. For my fifteenth birthday, my dad found out that Donald O'Connor was appearing at the Moulin Rouge on Sunset in Hollywood, and he organized a surprise of a front table for me and my boyfriend--and an orchid corsage. That same year some out of town friends of my grandparents in Nebraska went to Disneyland and wanted me to join them at the last minute. My dad was working, and so took me to the Van Nuys Airport and put me on a helicopter to Disneyland.

I adored those impulsive exploits of fierce abandon and courage in the face of impossibility, as we always were poor. My mother was more conservative with money but she also loved to have a good time. My family never took a vacation but we often went out to dinner--to Phil Ahn's Moongate or downtown to Chinatown, to the Red Barn for steaks with baked potatoes topped with sour cream and chives.

It was only later that I linked my own personality to my father's, when newly married at twenty, I went to the bank to take out two of the three dollars in my account to spend it at the House of Pancakes, an act my father would have understood.

Now I could hear him urging me, Go to Paris for chemo! Judas Proost, why not?

I didn't give two figs about saving money. For all I knew, with my lymph node metastases, I didn't have to worry about any future. If I had any money, I was going to spend it. There was no way I was going to die with money in the bank. I wanted to be in France, so, as I had two years before, I went to Paris.

CHAPTER 16

LADY DYNAMITE

*Lady Dynamite, let's dance quickly,
Let's dance and sing and dynamite everything!*

~ French anarchist song of the 1880s

Bald, weak, with a complexion the color of haricots verts, my heart might have been in France, but my body couldn't get there on its own. Adam came down from Sacramento to help me. Secretly I was glad to get him away from his cult for five weeks. Maybe he'd meet a stunning French girl and forget all that nonsense. Jason promised to be in touch with Grandma's caregivers, and to visit once in a while.

The flight to Paris was direct and uneventful, except for losing my black knitted cotton cap when I fell asleep and waking to the fact of my being bald in a public place. Olivier met us at Orly, looking shocked and dismayed. I had changed a lot in two months.

But I was back in Paris, with Olivier, and Adam too. I was so glad I had spent the money on our airline tickets, and of course I knew as a foreigner it would cost a lot to have chemotherapy in a country where the government pays for everything for its citizens. My HMO didn't charge me a cent for any of my extensive therapy in Los Angeles. So I was splurging big time. For me, it was Damn the torpedoes!

I couldn't wait to have a café au lait, but I feared it wouldn't taste the same. The chemo drugs had changed my taste buds. Nothing tasted like it should, or was worth eating. Most of the time I was so full of all the vitamin pills and supplements I took now that there was no room for food anyway.

When we got to the 3rd arrondissement, Olivier let me and Adam out on the corner with our bags while he parked the car. He didn't want anyone to see us together in case his wife could prove adultery in their divorce case. Olivier thought it convenient that Adam was there too, as he provided additional cover.

It wasn't easy for me to walk up the five flights of stairs. I remembered when I first climbed them not so long ago the day when Olivier invited me for lunch. I had been fit from dancing then, and happy, so I just flew up the steps. I thought the ancient apartment building was that much more charming and romantic without an elevator. Now I couldn't get my breath and had to pause several times to rest against the wide oak banister. Yet the apartment was so beautiful with the sun coming in the tall French windows, I knew the trip and the climb had been worth it. I sank onto the black leather couch, sweating and breathing hard. It was August and stifling. My blue knit sack dress was soaking wet. And I had to shyly take off my cotton hat; it too was wet and I felt suffocated.

"Adam, I put your bag in this little room off the kitchen, which will be yours. But if anyone asks, you must not say that Cherie is your mother, but your lover. We must be very careful," Olivier instructed the two of us, looking serious. He went to the windows and peered out.

"Oh please leave the windows open, I'm so hot!" I begged.

"The neighbors might see you. It is better that they do not," he said, closing the draperies.

Adam, anxious to explore the city and to escape the situation and hot apartment, borrowed Olivier's worn Plan de Paris, which he jammed into the back pocket of his jeans, and left, bounding back down the stairs with a badly pronounced, "Au revoir!"

Olivier went to the kitchen and began to take things out of the small refrigerator. "Tu veux quelque chose? Are you hungry, chérie? It is time to eat."

"Mind if I clean up first?" I struggled to my feet, and went towards the bathroom. The apartment was just as I remembered it from the spring. Olivier's wife had come and gone back to Nepal, but her things were still everywhere: her jewelry box, photos, perfume bottles, clothes, books and papers. I took notice of them all on my way to the bathroom.

I started running the water into the tub, putting in some drops of Delfine's Badaedas, wanting to cool off in a tepid bath. But after a while I realized the water filling up the tub was stone cold. There didn't seem to be any hot water at all. When Olivier came in to check on me, bringing the scent of sautéed onions with him, I complained about the lack of hot water. "Oh well the temperamental water heater must not be working again. Do you want me to boil some water on the stove?"

By this time I was already undressed and in the cold water, hoping to get cool and clean, but instead the hot flash turned into a chill and I started shivering. Olivier washed me quickly, and got me into his big art nouveau mahogany bed, where he piled on the blankets to stop my shaking, and went back to the kitchen. A hot flash, une bouffée de chaleur, struck again, and I threw off all the covers and lay damp and naked, sweating once more.

I gave Olivier some money for expenses, as his hours at the school were down to almost nothing and Adam and I were two people to feed. That afternoon he went shopping, and along with groceries, he brought back to the apartment seven hundred dollars worth of plastic miniblinds with which to cover all six of the tall windows that opened onto the street. "Those aren't pretty," I said. "The draperies go much better with the apartment. Plus blinds are noisy and clackety. Why do you want those?"

"For privacy. Please Cherie, do not go near to the windows. We do not know who is looking at us. Delfine has her spies."

The next day after bringing back a sack of hot croissants for breakfast from the bakery on rue de Temple, Adam took off for the Louvre. Olivier went to work at the French school, and I took a taxi to see the oncologist who would be in charge of my chemotherapy treatment two weeks later.

Shabby folding chairs, stacks of ancient torn magazines, and a giant tropical fish tank in the linoleum-floored waiting room, Dr Martin's office was not similar in the least to any doctor's office I had visited in the U.S. Dr Martin was somewhat unkempt, with long shaggy hair that needed washing. Once in the examining room, he instructed me to get undressed while he sat and looked at the medical file I brought, and then without benefit of a paper gown or any other modesty provision, he examined me. After checking my body, he asked me to take off my scarf and he looked at my bare scalp and my hands. He sat down again at his desk in the corner of the examining room while I got dressed, and made out his bill and instructions for the hospital.

―――

Adam felt immediately at home in Paris and was out most of the time. He bought a Pariscope listings magazine and checked and circled concerts, museums and discos he wanted to attend. He had a natural sense of direction and found his way around with ease. He didn't seem to be at all hampered by his lack of French. And after only a few days he had met some people to do things with. He told me anyway he preferred to be out as Olivier took up a lot of space, and I realized it was true. Sometimes it was exhausting to be with him. However I took up so little at the moment that I was pleased to have no responsibility for decisions, conversation, being entertaining.

Olivier seemed conflicted by our being there; happy, but very nervous. His teaching schedule finished early in the afternoon, and he usually went to the shops on his way home to buy provisions for dinner. Sometimes Adam would pick up some food items, but we saw him less and less as the weeks wore on. He had found the Paris contingent of his cult, and immediately became swallowed up by them and their activities.

Olivier and I were alone in the apartment most of the time, which suited me just fine when we made love, which we did at least once, and sometimes twice, a day. I had brought a special cap to wear in bed, which looked like a white baby's bonnet with a pink bow on the front, that I felt ridiculous wearing. I no longer wanted to have a light on or do it by daylight. Maybe in the dark we could both forget. But I sure still wanted to do it.

We went out sometimes, but always separately. He didn't want us to leave or enter the building together, or walk down his street at the same time under the eyes of the neighbors, who may have been on Delfine's side. His own friends all knew about me and the situation and came over for dinner parties, and they in turn invited us to their homes. Obviously the couple's friends had chosen up sides long ago. I supposed I was quite the novelty item of the summer. The conversations always centered around The Divorce, Olivier's strategy, the various testimonies that friends had to write, who was right, who was wrong, his lawyer. Olivier didn't listen to any advice; he had strong opinions about how to proceed and was furious with his wife, anger built up over many years, I imagined.

He had told his parents about me, and the first weekend I was there, we were invited out to their country house to spend the day. I was worried about meeting them, especially in the condition I was in. I didn't look or feel good, and I was the "other" woman to his conservative Catholic family. Although being bald and sick, I probably appeared less of a vamp and more sympathetic. But Olivier was confident that they would like me and be happy that we loved each other.

"Being good Catholics, my parents do not like divorce, but they will certainly like you," he assured me. "They really never cared for Delfine very much, but they supported her because of me. And now they will be happy to see how much you love me. Delfine and I never were in love like you and I are. They want me to be happy." This was something I understood very well, as I felt the same about my children. How could I ever not love someone who adored my son?

Outside of Paris past Fontainebleau was the little village where Monsieur et Madame de la Tour had a miniature chateau six hundred years old in the middle of the sunflower fields. They had purchased it decades ago, and Olivier and his four sisters had spent every summer of their childhood there.

We drove down a long allée lined with poplar trees and through crumbling stone gates, parking in front of a broad low building that Olivier said was the ancient stables. His mother and father came out and stood in front of the open doorway of the manor house, as Olivier helped me climb out of his little Renault.

I smiled, Olivier kissed his mother on each cheek, and she and I and Monsieur de la Tour shook hands, then Olivier shook hands with his father. "Bonjour, bonjour, enchantée, plaisir, oui, bien, il fait chaud...pas mal..."

Monsieur and Madame, in their late seventies, were elegant, slim, attractive, spry. They were dressed formally in colorless clothes which didn't reflect the heavy humid heat of the late summer morning. We sat under the weeping willow next to the tennis court and drank soft drinks without ice. When the conversation lagged, Olivier sprang up and offered to show me around the gardens and the chateau.

I admired his father's gigantic roses, the family portraits in the salon including several photos of Delfine, a sophisticated blond, the dusty antiques in the huge attic where Olivier and his sisters had played cache-cache around the many brick chimneys as children. I was appalled by the lone toilet in the house, in a dank dark closet under the stairs in the foyer with a mean box of those tiny thin pink sheets that pass for toilet paper all over France. The dining room downstairs and a bedroom upstairs were closed off as the one had collapsed into the other—the bedroom stone tiles, and the ceiling plaster and parquet floor of the dining room were in a crumbled heap probably just as they had fallen years ago.

Because Olivier was obviously uncomfortable around his parents and the one sister, Chantal, who had showed up for lunch and who never actually looked at me directly, we took a walk along the dusty road into the village. At least they all called it, le village, but it was nothing more than a few houses, no shop, café, or even a church. A woman working in the garden in front of her cottage hailed us. "Monsieur Olivier, bonjour!"

"Bonjour, Madame. Je voudrais presenter ma fiancée."

Her smile enveloped me with warmth, and we all shook hands. She insisted we come in and sit around the large table that completely filled the front room. I had noticed that this was very French, that where one ate was often the most important room in the house.

Madame, who had cleaned the chateau for Olivier's mother for decades, set down a tray of liqueurs, or digestifs, and we were soon joined by the rest of her family and several other neighbors. The conversation was gossip about people and events I didn't know, but all curious eyes were on me. The fact that the long married M Olivier had an American fiancée was big news.

It was blistering hot in the room. The front door was open but the air didn't move. I had also noticed that in France no one had so much as a fan to cool off in the hot weather. My white tee shirt was soaked, and I wanted to tear off my cotton hat to let my head breathe. I was sure everyone could see I had no hair anyway.

What must they be thinking? Why would Olivier want to trade the beauteous Delfine for me? Delfine was a tall, elegant woman with long blond hair. When she and Olivier were first married, she was a showgirl at the Folies Bergére. Later she started making trips to Nepal to research her university thesis, each time staying longer with less time in between journeys. For the past few years, she was in Nepal and Tibet most of the time.

Olivier said he was happy to have her gone, although sometimes he would accompany her for a short time to go trekking in the mountains of Katmandu like he did last spring. He said that he had been lonely and depressed for many years, and had contemplated suicide, but never divorce. "But now at last I know what love is," he told me. "And my family will be glad."

After all the food and drink and heat of the afternoon, I was exhausted. When we walked back to the chateau, I had to lie down. Olivier took off my shirt, wrung it out and found something dry for me to put on. I finally took off my hat and stretched out on the bed in the room that Olivier had slept in as a child. He lay down next to me and wanted to make love, but I couldn't in that bed and in that house of his parents, who believed in the sin of adultery.

During the next week in Paris I was alone most of the time. I had no energy to climb up and down those five flights of stairs very often. Once a day was my limit. I watched a lot of television, but usually I just sat on the couch. I couldn't look out the windows, because the blinds were always closed, but it was enough just to sit there.

Sometimes Adam and I would go to the neighborhood patisserie, Brocco, for café au lait. The shop was a fantasyland of marble, mirrors, ribbons and froufrou, gilt, and chocolate, which was sculpted into works of art. As we drank our coffee, we looked at the elegant displays that changed daily: life-sized lion masks, ladies' high-heeled slippers filled with bonbons, butterfly boxes—all crafted from gourmet chocolat du maison.

And once or twice I took the three of us out to a restaurant for dinner. I was spending a lot of money, but it didn't worry me, even though I had no income now that I couldn't work. I worried about a lot of things, but now the future wasn't one of them. I just wanted whatever it took to survive my therapy, mentally and physically.

The day came for my chemotherapy, and Adam wasn't at the apartment in time to take me. Olivier was going to leave from school and meet us at the hospital. I wasn't able to take the Métro alone. I waited nervously until almost the appointed hour, and then walked to the taxi stand in the Place de la République. I found where I was to go in the Hôpital Saint-Louis, but only after walking around and around looking for the entrance. The taxi had left me in the street, and I wasn't thinking clearly or able to discern where to go. By the time I had checked in for my blood tests, Adam and Olivier arrived together. With a man I loved on either side of me, the nurse started the IV with gloveless hands.

⁓

A few weeks later, I was back in Park La Brea, Adam had returned to the mountains of Sacramento, and Olivier was making plans to come to L.A. in two months when chemo was finished.

During the sixty days of my radiation treatments, Olivier drove me to the hospital every morning, and in the afternoon helped pack up all my things for disposal, storage and my move to Paris. His eyes seemed to glaze over during the lengthy sorting and careful wrapping of my various collections, such as the antique Victorian valentines, dollhouse miniatures and stacks of piano scores, and he seemed nervous and tense.

Before my treatment was officially finished, I had to see the radiation oncologist, who was the head of the department and had designed the treatment for me. He was an eccentric man with no bedside manner but with the highest recommendations and respect of his colleagues. He had also taken care of Jack's radiation therapy. Dr. Bruce tended to purple polyester pants and matching flowered shirts, but I didn't care as long as he knew what he was doing with my rads. Very gravely he said he had brought up my case at the department meetings, and everyone agreed with him that I should have the lymph nodes in my neck radiated too. I'd already had the few that were left under my arm zapped along with the radiation to my breast.

"The nodes of the neck are the most common target for breast cancer once it has metastasized," he told me.

"Won't that put me at further risk for lymphedema,

though?" I was paralyzed with fear of developing the "elephant arm" I had observed on so many women. And the risk of lymphedema never went away. As it stood, for the rest of my life I would never be able to have blood drawn or an IV on that arm, I had to fear cuts and insect stings, and was forbidden to lift and carry with my right arm. I didn't want to add to that risk. I agonized about it, how was I supposed to know what was best, I didn't go to medical school. But just as I followed my instincts and refused to take Tamoxifen because of how bad I felt on it, I said no to the extra radiation. Enough was enough. I wanted to move on and to start my new life in France. I would take my chances.

Dr Hadassian signed me off at my final checkup. It was scary to end treatment and just to be out in the world on my own, not to be actually fighting cancer anymore. What if there were still some cancer cells circulating around in my blood? "Well, my dear, we've blasted you with all the ammo there is. There would be nothing else to do for you anyway. We just have to have faith and trust, and go on living."

"So what's the prognosis, Doc?" I asked reluctantly, wanting to know, but afraid to hear it.

"With 5 out of 11 positive lymph nodes, and with your not being able to tolerate Tamoxifen, the odds are 24% that you'll make it to five years. But I don't see why you won't. I'm sure you are in that 24%." And he gave me a big hug and sent me on my way. Another door closed, or at least I hoped it was shut firmly.

The library gave me a Bon Voyage party with a French theme. And Olivier and I went to say goodbye to my mother in her board and care home. I hoped and prayed that Jason would be responsible with her. I had continued to visit her throughout my treatment, but never even tried to explain about my cancer. She looked with interest at my headscarves and my funny, hairless face with a greenish hue, but she didn't say anything. She didn't know me anymore, and seemed confused by Olivier, but smiled and enjoyed the visit. While she didn't know my name or her own, she knew what was important: that she and I loved each other. It had been so hard for her to know from the beginning that life would only continue to diminish without hope. Finally she was left in her own non-verbal world, but I knew, I could see it in her Irish eyes and crooked smile, that she loved me.

The word goodbye meant nothing to her. She thought she had always lived at Sunny Acres with Alma.

Christmas Eve Jason borrowed a friend's pickup and drove Olivier and me to the airport with my twelve pieces of luggage. Several employees had on jolly Santa caps, but everyone wore glum expressions.

CHAPTER 17

DIVORCE FOLLIES

We are never prepared for what we expect.

~ James A. Michener

In Paris, Olivier's friends in two small French cars picked us up. It wasn't snowing, but it was cold enough. I wore the black mink jacket Jack had bought me in Las Vegas years ago and a raccoon hat over my hairless head. Not only was the hat warm, but also from a little distance the fur looked like hair. Olivier and his friends dragged my bags up the five flights of stairs to his apartment.

The next day M and Mme de la Tour invited us to Christmas dinner at their large apartment on the other side of the Seine in the 6th arrondissement. It was awkward for everyone, but Olivier's parents were polite and gracious, and made me feel at home.

Madame offered me a package with a white silk scarf. "When I went to Lourdes recently on a pilgrimage, I had this especially blessed for you to speed your healing."

Moved, I kissed her on the cheek. "Merci, merci," as I put it around my neck.

His father flirted with me. I liked them both. I relaxed. I knew that Olivier was never relaxed around his family, and I was aware of his father's little digs and comments regarding his blighted hope in his son.

M de la Tour had been an important man from an important family. There were many pictures in the long hallway of him with various famous people, including De Gaulle. Having one son out of five children, he had put his hopes, money, discipline, and attention into Olivier, who had had all the advantages his four sisters weren't given. And then Olivier disappointed him. A classic situation. Olivier had never been ambitious or hard working. His childhood physical beauty, adult good looks and intelligence caused things to fall into his lap, and that was fine with him. He was spoiled and lazy. Despite all the fancy schools, world travel, and high expectations, Olivier, instead of being a doctor, lawyer, architect or CEO, at fifty years of age taught French as a second language part time. This was an embarrassment to his bourgeois family. And now he wanted a divorce to marry an American!

Olivier had filed for divorce. His wife was in Katmandu. I was moving in to live with him, but it was all wrong. In the apartment Olivier went into a frenzy of cleaning, vacuuming, washing, he wasn't still for a minute. I tried to make myself at home, but I was surprised that Delfine's things were still everywhere, and there was no place for mine. I had brought a small glass perfume bottle Jack had bought me in Venice, and there was no place of mine to put it. Olivier was paranoid, not wanting me to stand at the windows or answer the phone. Even more adamant than last summer when I had been there with

Adam for my chemotherapy, he refused to leave the apartment with me.

Divorce in France, while now legal and available, still was almost impossible if it were contested. And Delfine was fighting with all her might for property rights. There should have been no grounds for argument since Olivier's father had given him the apartment and the art nouveau antiques years before Olivier married Delfine, but in old-fashioned France, a rejected wife gets everyone's sympathy. Now the spacious five-room apartment in the heart of Paris was worth a fortune. Of course if there were children, Olivier would have had no hope of keeping what had been his for more than twenty years.

In French contested divorces, each party submits "evidence" in the form of depositions by friends as to how the couple behaved, what their relationship was like, who was "guilty." Consequently, any social interactions during the divorce proceedings are dominated by talk of who did what, who deserves what, and who has the most "witnesses" to their point of view. The judge can also request an inquest.

Olivier told me that in France the police have the right to come to the door in the middle of the night and examine who is sleeping where. They put their hands between the sheets of all the beds to see which ones are warm. The person of the opposite sex who is there at the time is written up as a "friend" or as a lover and the spouse as an adulterer. Contested divorces can take years. And if Olivier were proven an adulterer, he would lose everything. He knew Delfine was carrying on with a sherpa in Tibet, but how could he prove it?

Olivier was freaking out. Perhaps the reality of my living

there with him at last was too scary. And I was scared that all of a sudden I was sick and bald and alone in a foreign country in deepest winter. I gave up my elaborate dream of being a C & W bar diva, and concentrated on finding a library job. I had read in Library Journal that there was an opening in the library in the Pompidou Centre, and so I did my resume in French and filled out an application.

After only five days of living with Delfine's ghost (as well as her clothes in baskets under the bed and her cosmetics in the bathroom) and Olivier's fear of losing the apartment, my insecurities caused me to grab her photo off the mantel, stand in the open window in full view, and hurl it off the balcony with loud screaming. And then I pitched my Venetian perfume bottle after it. Why hadn't he thought of all of this before bringing me here, with twelve suitcases?

"Why, why do I have to live with her pictures staring at me and her underwear underneath the bed where we make love? What is the matter with you?"

"Your therapy and all of the drugs have made you crazy. You are no longer the Cherie I know. You need a psychiatrist!" he yelled at me.

"What did you think it was going to be like here, living with me? Didn't you think about that before bringing me across the world with all my things? I trusted you, I depended on you, I left everything for you because I love you. I can't live hidden away like a nasty secret. Why did I come? Oh why?" I sobbed.

"You are now too insane to understand. This is not the real Cherie who is speaking, but all of the cancer drugs that

143

changed you. I told you, Delfine has her spies!"

When he began flinging wine glasses to crash across the room, I shoved things into my bags frantically. I knew he wished I would disappear, that this was a nightmare he couldn't escape from. I had to get away. It hurt me so much that, finally, there I was, like I had dreamed and as we had planned, and he didn't want me after all.

"I have to leave. Please, if you care about me at all, help me. Take me to a hotel. I can't stay here anymore with your craziness." I went to the phone and called a hotel I had stayed in many years before with Jack.

Olivier dragged half of my bags down the stairs and into his Renault, and deposited them and me in the lobby of the Grand Hotel Moderne on the Left Bank. It was New Year's Eve. I was crying so hard, I could hardly see to push the luggage a few bags at a time into the elevator and up to my room. Because of the holiday, there was no clerk to help me.

The sixth floor chambermaid was annoyed that I propped open the elevator and blocked the hall with all my things. But when she saw my tears and my hairless head, and when I told her my fiancé had just brought me there, she hugged me like a mother. After she helped me lug the bags into my room, where there was almost no space for them, she brought me a bouquet of flowers and invited me to her house for New Year's dinner the next day. Her kindness made me feel so much better, and less alone, her warm offer of holiday hospitality really helped. I didn't need to accept. Instead, New Year's Day Olivier came over to the hotel and took me to dinner at an Alsatian restaurant nearby. It was dismal, grim, sad. He persuaded me to return to his apartment, and, not knowing what else to do,

I did, finding a huge flower display with a card, "Bienvenue a Maison" (Welcome Home) which I had probably paid for out of the money I was giving him. He was too paranoid and I was too much in need of security to suddenly have things go smoothly. We had another huge yelling fight. "Your illness has infected your mind," he screamed. "Now you are crazy!"

No one had ever talked to me that way before in my life. No one had ever said such mean things to me. In all my relationships over the years, now I realized how lucky I had been. I always knew my parents loved me and thought I was wonderful despite their own personal issues and marital problems, no man had ever cheated on me, and people I knew generally were polite. Great gifts. No one had yelled I was crazy and out of my mind and infantile and abusive, and I couldn't focus on the fact that Olivier was directing these comments at me with hate and anger.

I called Elizabeth, and Jean-Luc came over with his van (he was a professional musician and had a van to transport his equipment), and picked me up where I was standing in the snow in front of Olivier's building. He went upstairs to bring down my bags, and then drove me to the Place d'Italie and their apartment. Elizabeth and Jean-Luc gave me their room and they slept on the couch, the two children staying in the other bedroom. They said they didn't mind, but I felt so guilty. And all I did was cry. Finally I knew I had to be on my own, and so I decided to go to Evian and stay in my apartment. At least it was mine, or half mine anyway. And my partners weren't going there until May.

CHAPTER 18

DEPARTURES AND ARRIVALS

One's destination is never a place but rather a new
way of looking at things.

~ Henry Miller

After eight silent hours on the autoroute crammed into Olivier's little Renault along with those of my possessions that would fit, we arrived in the village of Lugrin outside of Evian-les-Bains. He left me his car, and I bumpedly drove him to the train station—it had been many years since I had driven a stick shift and clutch.

I appreciated having Olivier's car. Being out in the country that way, with no public transportation, I would have been totally stranded in the small village, which had a hotel and restaurant where I sometimes ate, a dreary bar, a tiny supermarket, a pharmacy, post office, and a beauty salon, of course the church and cemetery where Jack was buried.

My goal now was simply to recover from the cancer treatments and feel good again. I could do this so much better in my own space, without stress, with my good friends right next door. After all the drama in Paris, it felt so good to just relax.

Olivier came down by train on the weekends from time to time, but he was continually angry, and I guess I was too. We had a standing invitation to the Berengers' for Sunday dinner, but Olivier mostly scowled. Michel would greet Olivier with, "Ca va?" And Olivier always answered, "Ca ne va pas!" It made for tense conversation around the table. I just focused on Edith's delicious dinner while the others chatted small talk. There were usually other guests as well, such as Edith's father and Michel's mother Mémé, sometimes young friends of Floriane or Fabrice, sometimes employees of Michel's construction firm. Sunday dinner is important in France. I would help Edith in the kitchen, we'd have after dinner drinks and look at the lake, all of us full and satisfied, and then I drove Olivier to the station. Once or twice I went to Paris on the weekend, but then had to play the cat and mouse game of hiding from Delfine's spies.

I was glad to be able to go for walks up to the village and down to the lake. It was deepest winter and the countryside was lifeless. I kept telling myself that it was a lesson to know that the earth was only asleep, not dead. New life would soon push up from the ground, and I imagined the earth waiting, waiting for the right time. I had never lived anywhere with a real winter, and consequently never appreciated spring before. Easter flowers bloomed year-round in Los Angeles.

One morning I awoke to the quiet of the snow that had fallen in the night, making the wooden farm buildings, trees and bushes a lacey white Christmas card. I loved the clean white look of the world baptized in new snow. I wasn't used to seeing white; nothing is white in Los Angeles, least of all the trees. I stood on my back balcony staring at the cemetery and village church up the hill, and then on up to the white Alps, while breathing in the cold mountain air.

But by the time I went for my walk, the snow had begun to melt into the red earth of the road. As I trudged along, my eyes were glued to the ground trying to avoid deep puddles of milk-chocolate colored water. Pick-up trucks whizzed by and a man on horseback passed me, spraying the unmelted snow with muddy rain. The new snow now had the look of my morning cafe au lait. I had wanted to walk in a winter wonderland and I felt disappointed and stupid to be walking in mud, fearful of falling. But I was committed to a walk and I was going to continue until I saw a white unsoiled path that would lead me up through a stand of elegant trees, on which my steps would crunch in that delicious way and so I would be in that Hallmark card I had imagined.

Besides country walks, I entertained myself by building roaring fires in the fireplace. It got so warm inside I often had to open the balcony doors to the alpine air, especially as the hot flashes continued. But the fire was a living presence and company for me. When Floriane loaned me her television set, I watched TV and the fire all day and all night, with time outs to monitor the moods of the lake. I had never been in Lugrin in winter, and now I could see what Mémé meant about how the lake never looked the same way twice.

I played the French cassettes I had been collecting and tried to sing along. Charles Aznavour's *Hier Encore* made me think of the Beatles' *Yesterday*. What word contains more nostalgia? "Yesterday when I was young." That's usually what "yesterday" means—the good old days when the livin' was easy, when I was happy. The future is when we'll be happy again, and yesterday we were certainly happy, and today is only the transition, the holding area where we remember, and look forward to being happy again.

Sunday mornings I drove into Evian to the Catholic church, Our Lady of Assumption, with its altar built over an ancient pagan one. An Anglican priest ferried over each week from Lausanne to offer services in English in a side chapel. I bundled up as it was freezing cold in the church; generally there were few attendees. Clutching the prayer book with gloved hands, I always prayed for acceptance of my fate, whatever it might be. I felt blessed to be there with the old grey stones on the edge of the lake, and thankful.

Then I would go to the Berengers' for Sunday dinner. After one such fabulous feast, Michel asked me if I'd done the paperwork on the mortgage insurance.

"What mortgage insurance?"

"French law requires it. That way if something happens to the owner, the mortgage is paid off at the bank. Your half of the apartment should have been automatically paid off when Jack died."

"You are kidding! That would be fantastic. I've been so worried because I really can't keep making my half of the payments. And then I'd always have a place to live, even half the time."

"Bien, young lady, you should go down to the bank with your papers and check on it."

"You will always have a home here in Lugrin, Cherie. You will be welcome any time," said Edith, taking my hands and looking into my eyes, which made me fill up with emotion and tears. I didn't say it, but I thought that if the cancer were to come back, I would want to die in my beautiful apartment overlooking the lake. And then be buried with Jack in Lugrin's peaceful cemetery.

I was so happy to go into Evian to the bank the next day—not only did it give me something to do, but something positive to think about. And it turned out that Michel was correct. I had to supply faxes of the boys' signing off their inheritance rights and other documents, as under the inheritance laws of France the property goes to the surviving spouse and the children equally, but then I wouldn't have to worry anymore about the monthly mortgage, a huge relief.

In Lugrin, in the winter, there was really nothing to do alone, even if one felt well. The villagers worked hard, dug in for the winter, and those who could afford to, went skiing in the local resorts. I searched out all possible ways to entertain myself. I had no energy and didn't need much diversion, and the prospect of buying a new magazine in the village tabac was enough to make my day. I tried to pursue the idea of bus tours to various places, but everything was suspended until spring. I did find a poster for an Elvis convention in Evian, and I took Edith to that—almost an out of body experience.

One day when I hiked to the village for groceries, there was a flyer posted on the town hall bulletin board about gymnastics classes Tuesday and Thursday evenings. Needing exercise after all the past months of sitting around, I went up to the rec hall on the first night of the gym. It was icy cold, walking up the hill, and I was glad I had warmups, a parka, hat and gloves. The cows were kept in the barns now, but when

I passed them in the yards on my walk up, I was amazed to see their white fur had grown long and curly for the winter.

The village women were surprised to see me and even more astonished when I took off my hat. But once the class got started, I was just one more woman. In democratic France there was often an "animator" instead of a "teacher," as everyone was considered equally knowledgeable. Slender Beatrice with very short black hair was the animateuse tres formidable of the gym class. We exercised with balls and hoops and sticks and did movements I had never seen before, all to French folk music and old French music hall songs. I was happy spinning hoops in the circle of women to Yves Montand's "La Bicyclette." This class was my salvation from boredom and loneliness. It was the closest I had come to dancing in so many months.

Mardi Gras was coming up and there was to be a big parade in Evian, with all the clubs, groups, and municipal organizations participating, and Le Gym de Lugrin would too. It was decided that we would be Dalmatians, and discussion over our costumes took up the first few minutes of every workout session. We used white nylon flight suits with attached hoods, to which we glued black spots, and wore red collars. Olivier came down from Paris for the parade, and helped me put on my white face makeup with black dots of greasepaint. Under the suit, I wore four layers of warm clothing, and so I felt like a tightly packed sausage as our group waited behind the water skiing club up by the Palais de Congres for the signal to start down the hill.

Parading through all the narrow streets took hours but it was enormous fun to be completely incognito for the first time in my life. Several Dalmatians did crazy things—running into butcher shops and begging for sausages, and generally acting silly—and how freeing it was. It was beautiful to be outside on the cold March day, looking down at Lac Léman and up at the snowy Alps. Who ever knew I'd be a dog in a French parade?

Olivier stood in the crowd and snapped photos as the groups marched past, and afterwards we went to the big dinner fête in the Evian Convention Center, sitting at a large table with families we didn't know.

We felt closer to one another after that day. Maybe because Mardi Gras had been so much fun for us both and a distraction from trying to get along. We made plans for me to return to Paris in April, as Sam and Susie were coming to stay in the apartment on vacation and I had to leave anyway. In the meantime, Delfine, back from Katmandu, had managed to get Olivier thrown out of the apartment and she had moved in. We would have to stay with Isabelle and Jacques, his best friends, in their place in Belleville, the 10th arrondissement.

So I moved back to Paris with my suitcases and duffle bags. Olivier and I slept in Jacques' study, and I went to the garment district and bought two rolling racks for my clothes which went in the hallway.

Jacques and Isabelle were nice about it, but I could see it was annoying for them to have us there. I got in trouble for not shutting the toilette door tightly (in the U.S. the habit generally is to keep it open when unoccupied), or leaving a pot unwashed in the kitchen. Olivier tried to clear his computer off the dining table each evening before they arrived home, but didn't always succeed. Olivier, who had gotten laid off when the French school closed, did some interior decoration work for Jacques and Isabelle in exchange for our staying there. He also went every day for a retraining course in computers, paid for by the government. I bought groceries and tried to be a good guest. There was no getting around it; the situation was awkward for everybody.

One hot afternoon we went to the Marché des Puces, the flea market, to look at wedding rings. At the jewelry and antique stalls we both tried some on, but I didn't like any of them. I was no longer in the mood to think about marriage.

We heard music, though, and I perked up. Following our ears, we found a small bar full of people dancing to a live accordion band. Olivier was a good sport, one of his best qualities, and we joined in the Bal Musette, dancing as people had danced in Paris, probably in that same place, for the past hundred years. Olivier was embittered with his divorce proceedings and I felt displaced and unwanted. We took a lot out on each other. But during that afternoon hour in the bar, it was new again.

Foolishly I had imagined that living with Olivier would be like living with Jack, that we would each watch out for the other and put our partner first. I was learning that to Olivier, he was always first and foremost, and I should prioritize the same. After all, his whole life had taught him that.

When our time was up in Belleville with Isabelle and Jacques, we moved to Olivier's parents' apartment, in their bourgeois neighborhood near the Observatory on the Left Bank. His parents left Paris to spend the summer in their chateau in the country as they did every year, and offered us lodging. I hoped that without the stress of living with other people, maybe we could work things out between us. I so wanted to live in Paris and continue the plans that Olivier and I had made more than a year ago. There was no danger of our marrying, as he wouldn't be divorced for many years.

I had been to the parents' apartment before, of course, for dinner. I never had a good look at it in broad daylight, and moving in with all my suitcases was a shock. The apartment had fabulous bones, being over a hundred years old and art nouveau. The majestic hallway was curved, and all the doors leading off of it were curved too, with yards of fancy carved moldings. There was a grand salon with balconies, a dining room overlooking a little chateau on the grounds of the Observatory, three bedrooms, a grand piano, a large kitchen and butler's pantry, two bathrooms, and a grotty toilet.

But it hadn't been painted in sixty years! No improvements had ever been made since they lived there. This was the original deal. Which meant peeling paint, ancient plumbing fixtures, tarnished silver and broken down furniture.

Olivier and I had to sleep in the dining room at his parents' request. There was a narrow couch and he brought alongside it a single bed. This was an enormous concession on their part, as they were ultra conservative and ultra Catholic. But even though they were hospitable and understanding to me, I felt like an intruder, like an American siren who had broken up their son's marriage of twenty years, and I suppose, that's what I was. Throughout the apartment there were family photos on display, and several of Delfine.

The wonderful piano in his father's study, which I played daily, made up for everything else. I even found some coffee-stained sheet music signed by Maurice Ravel in the piano

THE CHURCH OF TANGO

bench. When I mentioned the find to Madame, she nodded, saying, "Ah, oui... Maurice."

We had stayed two months with Isabelle and Jacques, and now we were going to stay two months at his parents'. It was August again, the only month I hate in Paris. Last August I was having my chemo and the city was the antithesis of all the love songs. The only people in town were the tourists wearing shorts, many businesses were closed, and there was no place to cool off. At least this August I wasn't suffering like last year, although I was still very weak. My hair actually looked kind of cute, as it had grown in kinky and I had bleached all one inch of it blond at the beauty shop in Lugrin.

The parents came to dinner as guests in their own apartment. The tension grew as we sat around the big dining table set with tarnished monogramed silver and embroidered linen napkins. Olivier brought in the soup in a lovely old tureen and began to ladle it out.

"Beautifully prepared and presented. Perhaps you should alter your focus," said Monsieur de la Tour. "With all of your advantages—the prep school in England, the university, all that we gave you, and you never made anything of yourself."

Madame didn't pay any attention, having heard it a thousand times before I supposed, and I just stared at my plate, feeling uncomfortable. Olivier refilled the wine glasses and then brought in the fish course.

In the salon after dinner, Olivier chatted with his mother while Monsieur de la Tour and I flipped through a family photo album. Stopping at a picture of blond curly-headed Olivier at three years of age with his four older sisters, I remarked,. "He hasn't changed a bit, has he?"

"No, he has not," chuckled Monsieur.

My attention fell on the bookshelf behind Monsieur, where *"The Little Prince"* sat. I pulled it down. "Olivier looked like this!" I said. Opening the cover, I saw that the book was signed by Antoine St-Exupéry, the author. I didn't say that Olivier had also been treated like a little prince who now felt entitled.

As Olivier brought in demi-tasse on a tray the conversation turned to the following week, as Monsieur et Madame's time in the country was coming to an end. Olivier and I had to leave and find another place to stay. He wanted to return to Jacques and Isabelle's until a judge ordered Delfine to vacate his apartment. He had finished the retraining classes but still hadn't found a job. I was paying for everything and sleeping on a couch in a dining room like a bad relation. When we were alone, washing up in the kitchen, I complained. He retorted, "At least you aren't paying any rent!"

I couldn't take it anymore. I just wanted to bolt, to run all the way back to my old life in Los Angeles, and I went over to the studio apartment of his friend Claude to escape. I had the keys because that was where I got my mail since Olivier didn't want it to come to his address or to his parents'. The apartment was almost always empty, as Claude used it only when he came into town from Provence.

I sat on the couch for the whole day and night, not eating, drinking, or doing anything but crying. My despair was total. For three years I had loved this man completely. During that time I had lost my gorgeous house of happy memories, my health, my mother to Alzheimer's and my children had given up their arts careers and left home. I could survive all those things if Olivier loved me, if we could be together in a healthy supportive way. Truly nothing else mattered. But now I saw it was my fantasy, not reality. Olivier and I could never have a healthy relationship. He lived in his own world and was incapable of understanding mine. I knew deep inside that this was the end.

At last I called Olivier to come and get me. My survival instinct won out. I had no strength to move. I was in shock and felt I was dying. I was completely dehydrated and developed a bladder infection. That desperate and lonely day was one of the lowest points of my life. Olivier hadn't a clue, and he was as furious as hell.

Even Olivier's own mother had said to him that my husband had been a man, and I couldn't be happy with a boy. What Olivier had loved about me was how much I had loved him; Narcissis-like he found his reflection in my eyes irresistible. When he confessed he had never been loved so much in his life, I thought it was probably sadly true. I was adept at loving, but now I realized that possibly loving Olivier was easier from another country, as maybe Delfine had discovered long ago. Now after three years of passion and pain, all my dreams had run out.

It was time for me to return to Los Angeles and try to get my old job back at the library before my unpaid sickleave expired, to try to salvage my life. I left ten suitcases of belongings behind and went home.

CHAPTER 19

CHATEAU RODNEY

A happy family is but an earlier heaven

~ George Bernard Shaw

Chateau Rodney's architecture was not the least bit French. It was a typical Los Angeles apartment building of the '20s, pseudo Spanish-Monterrey style with wooden balconies around a U-shaped courtyard. Rodney is the name of the street on which we lived in the Los Feliz district to the east of the Hollywood sign; Los Feliz is pseudo-Spanish for "the happy ones."

What a stroke of luck it was, even after weeks of hard work, to find the apartment. I was staying with friends in Hancock Park, and I had given myself a time-line of two weeks for medical checkups and tests, two weeks to get a job, two weeks to buy a car and find an apartment.

The apartment search I took on like a full-time job, working seven days a week calling ads, driving by possibilities, making appointments. Park La Brea was not an option. I had learned my lesson. Now I only considered one neighborhood, my old one, the one I had happily lived in all my adult life, so

THE CHURCH OF TANGO

that made it easier and harder at the same time. At the end of the two weeks, I saw a simple Apartment For Rent sign stuck in the grass of an old courtyard building one block from the library where I soon would be working again. It was perfect but still I had to go back and look two or three times more before signing the lease. The third time, after measuring for my Persian rug and grand piano that were in storage since last year, I sat on the closed lid of the toilet, looking at the old cracked 20's tile in gold and maroon, and cried with my head in my hands, huge sopping tears. This wasn't how my life was supposed to have turned out in so many ways. The total unexpectedness of renting this apartment back in Los Angeles hit me like an atomic blast. I never planned this, and yet there I was.

The apartment had what I wanted—a big living room, high ceilings, and places to walk to. It also had arches, stained glass, and an upstairs like my old house. I loved the old palm trees lining the street, so tall and stately, yet leaning when the Santa Anas blew. They knew how to survive. I loved how they looked from my balcony at sunset, how the sun caught the tips of the frilly fronds and made them appear on fire, something I loved seeing out my windows at Park La Brea too. Their silhouettes against the orange western sky were just like the images on postcards from exotic holiday destinations, but this was my view, in downtown Los Angeles. Still, moving in was a shock. All my furniture, at least the things I'd saved in storage after my house sale, didn't fit. The tiny kitchen had no room for the refrigerator, which had to go on the back porch. The apartment was like a dollhouse, a miniature version of my old house a few blocks away, in era, style, details; it seemed to mock the loss of my old life.

I guessed about and glimpsed the neighbors, but our hours were different and we rarely crossed paths. That's normal in Los Angeles apartment life anyway. Most of the tenants were in the entertainment industry and toured or worked odd hours and we zigged and zagged around each other back by the garages as we came and went. We waved at each other through the stained glass bay window when I sat at the piano, and as we read on our balconies. We began inviting each other over for drinks. After a while something special happened at Chateau Rodney. Somehow the beauty of the architecture and the vibrations of the history and the energy of all the people who had lived there over the decades caused a weird phenomenon practically unheard of in L.A. to occur among all of us—we bonded. I felt less lonely than I had in a long time.

Once I had arrived back in L.A. I followed up Michel's information on my French apartment's mortgage insurance. What I had to do now was to prove that Jack was diagnosed after we bought it with Sam and Susie, not before. I asked Dr Carson if he would move back the date a few weeks on the form to be signed, and he was furious, insulted even. I didn't know what difference it would make to him and his ethics, Jack was gone anyway, as dead as dead could be. We didn't buy the apartment with a plan of cheating anyone by his dying. We didn't even know about the mortgage insurance. Would it have been so bad to back date his diagnosis after all that had happened?

So instead I got out the papers from the Tijuana hospital and wrote down the doctor's name and license number. Then I went to a stationery store in Korea Town and ordered a rubber stamp. I filled out the French insurance papers, signed Dr Mario Rodriquez' name and stamped them with the official-looking seal. I messengered the forms and lots of other paperwork to the bank in Evian.

When it was all official, I emailed Sam and Susie that we needed to meet; that I had good news to share, that the insurance had paid off. They suggested a fancy bar in Beverly Hills. I was surprised when I got there that there was a stranger sitting at the table with them. Three cocktail glasses sat empty in front of them. Sam introduced "their friend and lawyer, Stuart." When the waiter arrived I ordered a Kir, and the other three ordered another round.

"You guys know that I've had a hard time financially since Jack's death and my own cancer. Now the obligatory mortgage insurance has paid off my half of the apartment!"

Complete silence.

"I had to file a lot of paperwork in France by mail and jump through some hoops. But, isn't it great? I have been so concerned how I was going to keep on making the payments every month."

"Yeah," Susie said, "we sure can use the break ourselves."

"Excuse me? I don't understand. My half of the mortgage was paid off with Jack's death. And now despite everything, at least I can have a roof over my head for half the time." I smiled lamely.

Stu now piped up. "Correction. One half of the

mortgage, taken out by all four parties, was paid off, effectively reducing the balance by half. The whole partnership as a group benefits by the debt reduction under California law."

"But Sam! Susie! We've been friends for years! After I phoned, you hired Stu? Surely there's a moral right here that doesn't depend on California law? Jack paid for my half with his life, the ultimate price!"

"Stu is advising us all that both of our payments are now halved," said Sam.

"You're kidding, right? If you do this you're taking away my only chance to hang on in Evian."

"It's the law," Stu said.

I stared at all of them and heaved to my feet, accidentally catching and pulling the tablecloth with me, spilling the drinks into Sam, Susie and Stu's laps as I ran out of the restaurant, crying.

The next week I received a letter from Stuart, presenting an offer from Sam and Susie to buy my half of the apartment. It was less than Jack and I had originally paid, and of course we had purchased furniture and made all those monthly payments, so I just tried not to think about the loss. The loss of the dream of living in France, visiting Lugrin and Jack's grave, the Berengers', was much worse than the financial loss. I had no alternative; I had to let go.

⸻

Olivier passed through my thoughts often, and when I got nostalgic remembering the early days of our romance, I fast-forwarded in my head to the painful ending, when he let me go without complaint.

I was playing the piano before leaving for work one morning when the telephone rang. "Comment-vas tu, Cherie?" It was Olivier.

"I am surviving, working, living. What do you want?"

"Oh Delfine has been temporarily awarded the apartment while the judge is making up his mind if it belongs to me or not, and so, I bought a ticket to Los Angeles!"

"What?"

"I have no job and have been staying with my parents. I thought I could go there and we could try again. I love America! I want to be an American!" he chuckled. "Maybe far away from France we can make it work."

"Well, ah, well… when?" I was astounded at the thought of Olivier at Chateau Rodney.

"Within a fortnight. I can not wait to see your 'enchanted cottage." I had told him in an email that my apartment was a miniature version of my old house a few blocks away, and that it was like a dollhouse, an "enchanted cottage," *une maison enchantée*.

I was back to work at the library full time, even though the doctor told me it was too soon, but I didn't think I had any choice. Maybe it would be easier with Olivier. Maybe we could rekindle the embers. Maybe away from Paris and all of his problems we could make it new again.

CHAPTER 20

LA VIE DU CHATEAU

Paradise is exactly like where you are right now...
only much, much better

~ Laurie Anderson

Olivier arrived in the middle of October, two months after my return. Part of me resented that I did all the work of finding an apartment, unpacking everything from storage, and getting settled all by myself in August, to make the cottage ready for his arrival. If he had to come, I wished he had come with me and helped me. At the time, he was just angry.

I picked him up from Air France with his clothing and two big boxes of books and CDs. He loved the apartment and that I had a computer and the internet, and cable TV. I was stunned he was there in Chateau Rodney, but hoped for the best.

Since I was gone ten hours every day to work, and always arrived home exhausted, it was a relief to know that Olivier could do the shopping and cooking. I hadn't been eating well as I was too tired after work to care. I gave him the money to buy the food as well as pocket money, and hoped that once he was sorted out he would look for some kind of work.

There was a private French primary/secondary school just a few blocks away that perhaps could use him as a tutor. He was also very handy and maybe could do some household repairs and maintenance around the neighborhood. I showed him the bulletin board at the market where he could post notices. I gave him my car whenever he wanted it, which wasn't often.

He found the French channel on TV, and spent a lot of time on the internet. Every day he read the L.A. Times out on the balcony, making lists of movies he wanted to see; I never had the energy or time to do more than glance at the headlines. Going to the movies wasn't on my calendar.

However, every year there was a staff Halloween party downtown at Central Library, a gorgeous historic Art Deco building. And Olivier and I went dressed as the King and Queen of France, with wigs and makeup and beauty spots. He knew perfectly how to toss his lace handkerchief and prance like Louis XIV. It was the most fun I had had in a very long time, maybe since Mardi Gras in Evian when I was a Dalmatian. Dressing up was liberating. I had so wanted to be French; maybe this was the best I could do.

Jason wasn't working either. Construction had used him up. He was no longer at Benny's house and was couch-surfing two weeks here and two weeks there. He took occasional ballet classes and talked about returning to a ballet company or teaching, but I was worried that he had been out of the game too long. Three years without daily ballet was a long time. I was very concerned about him, my beautiful, brilliant boy. No work, no place to live. A young man who had been on the ladder of success, he had been floundering since Jack's death. I had always believed in tough love, but now it was time to step in. It was cramped and somewhat awkward, but I asked him to stay with Olivier and me at Chateau Rodney on condition that he find a job, any job, within a month. It was November and lots of businesses hired extra help for the holidays.

He started work within a couple of weeks at Trader Joe's, had running around money, and wasn't at the apartment often. Whenever he was, he was respectful and gave Olivier space. I knew it was hard on him, on me too, but the truth was, I loved having Jason around after not seeing him much in the past few years. Everyone loved Jason and his sense of humor, sparkling personality and good nature. He quickly made friends with all the neighbors, unlike Olivier. Maybe Olivier wasn't so happy to have Jason there, but it was my apartment and my son. The two men kept a safe distance from each other in the small space.

Olivier though didn't seem to be making any progress with getting part time work. "I can't work, it's illegal," he justified.

I had been thinking about it, a possible solution, and an exhausting probable future if he couldn't carry some of the financial weight. "What about if we get married?" I said. "We can go to Tijuana, get a Mexican divorce, and then get married. The United States recognizes Mexican marriages and divorces. Then you can get your Social Security card, green card, and a job. What do you think?"

He looked flabbergasted. I was too at the boldness of the idea, particularly when I no longer yearned to marry him. I was learning that when desperate, I came up with desperate solutions. When I was cornered, I tried to box my way out. On my next day off, we drove down to Tijuana. I didn't want to do this, I felt sad and depressed about it, but if he would get a job and contribute to the expenses, maybe it would be worth it. I hoped it would be worth it. He got his divorce in a lawyer's office, and then the same lawyer married us. We went to the corner bar for margaritas, and mariachis serenaded us. I paid of course for everything. When we got back to L.A. we filed the papers for his change of status. We didn't tell anyone but Jason. I just didn't feel like announcing the wedding or celebrating. I understood better now why perhaps Delfine lived across the world from her husband.

Being a "house husband" suited him in that he could stay home all day doing nothing. He loved American culture, and no longer cooked the delicious French meals he had prepared for me in France. Instead it was fast food, frozen food, certainly not French food.

One night the three of us went to the Groundlings, an improvisational theater group on Melrose. We were early and sat in the second row. During the show the director of one of the skits approached Olivier to ask him a few questions to set up the next skit. "What is your name, sir?"

"Olivier."

Noticing his accent, the director asked, "Where are you from?"

"France!"

"And what do you do, Olivier?"

"Me? I do nothing!"

The skit then started. An actor lay on the stage as if he were dead. More of the cast came on stage and tried to question the man, who wouldn't move.

CHERIE MAGNUS

"What are you doing?" a woman asked him, annoyed at his just lying there.

"I do nozing. I am *French!*"

The audience roared, Jason and I looked at each other with our sides splitting. We looked at Olivier who did not get it at all. But I got it.

December came, Jason was working a lot and out with his friends and wasn't around much. Olivier was nervous and angry, I was exhausted and resentful. The truth was I was slightly afraid of him, of his temper and his shows of violence in France. He was big and strong and on edge. We never talked. I couldn't sleep. There was incredible tension. I insisted that we go for a session with my psychologist, a woman I had been seeing whenever possible ever since I became a passenger on the cancer train. We made the appointment and unbeknownst to me, Olivier wrote her a sixteen page letter of all my faults. When we arrived at her office, he refused to sit, and lectured for fifteen minutes about how abusive I was, that I was insane since my chemotherapy, there was no getting along with me. Both Karen and I sat listening with our mouths open. When he finished his diatribe, he stormed out. I had hoped Karen could help us smooth things over, but she was shocked at his narcissistic behavior and refusal to talk. She said, "I never say this, but in this case I have to declare that he is 'crazy' and there is no chance for a healthy relationship with him." I left her office without any hope. He wrote her sixteen pages and wouldn't talk to me.

When I got home from the library a couple of days before Christmas while Jason was still at work, Olivier was watching TV, and I knew that no matter what, I couldn't do it any more.

We went into the kitchen to prepare dinner. "Olivier, can we talk? I am not happy. Are you? We have to discuss some things." He had taken out a knife and the cutting board.

His answer was to ram the knife into the kitchen wall. He jerked it out and jammed it in again, hard. Then he began to yell in French. I was so frightened I had no idea what he was saying, but it didn't matter. I couldn't do any more than what I had done. I couldn't try any harder. I was done with him and the situation one more time.

I screamed back, "Enough! You have to leave. Go back to France, or somewhere else. We can't do this any more."

"I have no money," he yelled, his handsome face contorted with rage.

I went upstairs and dug deep in my closet and took out $1,000 from my money box. "Take this and get out."

In angry silence we packed up his things, and I drove him to the airport, all the while afraid of him, afraid he might explode again. But maybe he knew the situation was impossible and was glad someone had finished it. I let him off at Air France and he slammed the door. That was it.

The next night was Christmas Eve. I walked the four blocks to church for the midnight service with such relief, so happy to be alone. I just prayed Thank you, Lord, thank you. No one to criticize me, no one to complain, no one to please, and no one to support.

Jason and I had a quiet Christmas Day and Adam gave me the gift of a long telephone call. Jason said he would give me a present the next day, but I had already received what I needed: peace. Before we both went to work the following day, Jason drove me to the animal shelter and we picked out a small tortoise-shell cat who we named Phoebe. "Mom, I knew you needed a cat," Jason explained. He was right.

Whenever I missed Olivier or was lonely after that and entertained thoughts of communicating with him, I just stared at the two holes in the kitchen wall. And cuddled Phoebe.

Trader Joe's liked Jason and so kept him on after the holidays. We talked about his living with me and we agreed on a deadline of six months for him to save enough for his own apartment. Meanwhile he paid me token rent. Spring was coming. For my birthday in March. I wanted to have a get-together of my old friends but since the Chateau Rodney apartments were so small, Marisol, the beautiful actress next door, volunteered to co-produce the party and people could flow between our two units. She didn't have a rug over the hardwood floor, and so we could dance at her place. When they heard of the party plans, Joe, and Derek, a vice-president of an important PR firm in Beverly Hills on my other side, thought it would be fun to celebrate the Spring Equinox, and would I mind if they invited a few friends? The idea caught on around the building. Luckily Ted was back from his musical tour, Aimee's family was visiting her from San Francisco, and Steve, a screen writer, and Cynthia, who worked in television, loved any excuse to haul out their gas barbeque.

Party night 150 people boogied through all six apartments, the courtyard overflowed with wine, beer and soft drinks in tubs of ice, makeshift tables held potluck food and bowls of sangria. Twinkle lights and Chinese lanterns glittered everywhere around the balconies, across the courtyard, and through the trees. Nancy and her husband were there, as well as Jason.

There were three pianos in the six apartments and music and singing segued from one to the other as if a contrapuntist had planned a polyphonic concert. Professional friends of Ted sang old torch songs and show tunes around one piano or another while he or I played. People danced everywhere. Speeches were spoken from various balconies, and strangers were in and out of all six bathrooms. Marisol had made me a cake, and there I was blowing out the candles while a hundred people I didn't know sang "Happy Birthday" outside my front door.

The old cliché that you can't choose your family but you can choose your friends didn't apply to me. I loved my only family—my two sons—so much, and I also loved my neighbors who I didn't choose either.

Maybe I no longer had a pied-a-terre in France, but I was glad to live at Chateau Rodney in Hollywood. Following the auspicious celebration on my birthday the first year I lived there, with Marisol, Steve, Cynthia, Aimee, Ted, Derek and Joe, we had solstice/equinox gatherings every quarter, went river rafting together, took fieldtrips to the theater and art galleries, did communal gardening projects. We watched each other's cats. We approved and disapproved of each others' dates and love affairs. When one of us had a belly-dancing gig, we all sat around with our coffee cups and critiqued her act in the early morning light of the garden. A friend of a friend was a balloon man, and he was wont to show up at all hours whether there was a party or not with his balloon apron and made us balloon palm trees and balloon hearts pierced by balloon arrows.

Each big event inspired new ideas during the post mortems. Let's do a Romeo and Juliet night with spotlights on the roof, moving between the balconies!

Great, we can highlight famous scenes from Shakespeare and other plays with the audience watching from the courtyard below.

Hey, next Christmas let's rent a snow machine! We can have snowball fights and a snowman contest!

Imagine the perfect wedding we could have here! OK, who wants to get married?

Steve and Cynthia bought a plastic wading pool and kept it full all summer, while we all joked about our new amenity at the Chateau, cooling our heels and waving around our martinis expansively.

Whether it was a Thanksgiving potluck, Christmas carols while toasting marshmallows around the flaming portable barbeque, Easter brunch with an egg hunt, cocktails in the courtyard, or just a gripe session, you could always find a warm hug or a cold beer at Chateau Rodney. Because I was the oldest, and also maybe because I was the only one with a day job and a structured schedule, I was the official Mom of us all, and I loved it. I missed being a mom.

Now I enjoyed emailing my neighbors from the other side of a wall, simply yelling someone's name when needing to talk, joking about knocking doorways through so that all the apartments connected from the inside—we were always connected.

When Princess Diana died, we made an altar.

When Derek and Marisol saw me crying in my dining room one night after my mother died in the board and care home, they burst in my unlocked front door to comfort me with hugs and gentle words. And of course the whole building was there at her wake at the House of Pies two blocks away.

My earliest memory was of my mother singing "Toora Loora Looral" to me, I must have been barely three, but I remember that as she rocked me and sang, my heart almost burst with something I didn't understand, and strange tears washed my cheeks. Marisol sang it at the House of Pies.

Thank goodness for my Chateau Rodney family. I always knew that because of having no siblings, cousins or aunts, I would be alone at my mother's funeral, especially as she had been in board and care for years and had lost her friends when her mind went. So Jason was there, and my friends. Adam didn't make it down from the compound.

Normalcy returned to my life. I worked full time at the library, attended my church a few blocks away, had a social life with my old friends and my new neighbors. I enjoyed being the dance critic for a local newspaper with house seats for every visiting dance company. How wonderful to be able to invite friends to join me for performances from around the world, a way to reciprocate their kindnesses of the past few years. Jason kept his bargain and saved enough to rent his own studio apartment in a recycled Budist monestery that was very Old Hollywood, and he got himself a cat.

Life was good. The Chateau community of such different souls was something so unusual it was almost otherworldly. I struggled even at the time to tell people about how we lived together, supported each other, had so much fun, because unless you had seen it with your own eyes you couldn't believe it. The magic was there—is probably still there—just when I needed it the most. The convergence of the planets or whatever it was over Chateau Rodney, allowed me to carry on with my life, shattered by circumstances, and to be almost happy.

What I missed was dance. And so when I saw that there were Argentine Tango lessons through the Learning Annex in West Hollywood, I signed up for eight classes. The teacher was an American woman who had made many trips to Buenos Aires. She taught social tango as opposed to the stage tango shows and movies I had seen before. Show tango was choreographed, and full of lifts and tricks and spectacular moves. Social tango was improvised and based on the embrace and the connection between the man and the woman, unlike any other ballroom dance I had ever experienced. I didn't need choreography, and I loved connection. Who knew then that the tango would change my life?

CHAPTER 21

SOLO TANGO IN BUENOS AIRES

The tango is man and woman in search of each other. It is the search for an embrace, a way to be together...The music arouses and torments, the dance is coupling the two people defenseless against the world and powerless to change things.

~ Juan Carlos Copes, dancer and choreographer

What was the tango, anyway? I had danced all my life but I didn't know the answer to that question, even after my eight lessons. I knew tango meant more than a dance, certainly more than a (slow slow quick quick slow) ballroom exhibition, a campy movie moment, or a Broadway show. I wanted to experience the legendary dancers' dance and all that tango meant. On my next ten days of vacation from the library, I made a pilgrimage to Buenos Aires. ("Pilgrimage" is commonly used by tango dancers to explain why they travel to Argentina to dance: it can be a religious experience.) Knowing no one in Argentina and no Spanish, I was lucky enough to hook up with a tour of dancers I found on the internet.

I still hadn't recovered my strength after my cancer treatments, and I was working full time. At night when I walked home to Chateau Rodney, I just praised God that I had survived another day. Yet I managed to drag myself over to tango classes in West Hollywood. I was also writing a lot, and along with the dance reviews, articles and book reviews in professional journals, I wanted to try my hand at writing travel pieces. Buenos Aires would be a great place to start.

In an elliptical way, the tango made me think of Jack. We had danced it together, albeit the American Ballroom tango taught in the States. Jack was a gringo from the getgo. Born and raised in Los Angeles as I was, his roots were Norwegian, his philosophy and outlook very U.S. of A. His tall and slim, blond-blue-eyed good looks and Brooks Brothers suits marked him better than his passport. A product of public schools and a graduate of UCLA and UCLA Law School, he wasn't elitist but he was elegant and had a natural grace. Athletic and an accomplished sportsman, he had learned to dance rock 'n roll in college, but when he met me he was inspired to dance more and enrolled at Arthur Murray's, discovering he was a closet Latin. The rumba, cha cha, and tango were his dances. He was shy and I suspect he would have had a problem with the sweaty, intimate close embrace of Argentine Tango with anyone but me.

Tango permeated the air of Buenos Aires--tango art and history, the dance of politics, the music of extinct German bandoneons, a 24-hour Tango TV channel, dancers on the streets, tango clubs two per block, altars to the saint of tango, Carlos Gardel. As far as I was concerned, the city could just as easily have been called Tango Aires. For a tanguera wanna-be like me and the other American women I met on the trip, it was paradise.

Buenos Aires was known as the Paris of South America, perhaps because a lot of the city's architecture emulates La Belle Époque. If you squinted your eyes you might think you were in Paris if you didn't know better: the French windows, balconies, wrought iron, sculptures of large buxom women over doorways. Elegant cupolas popped up on rooftops all over the city's skyline, stamping the city as somewhat European and indefinably Buenos Aires. To me, knowing and loving Paris so well, Buenos Aires was surreal, a distorted dream of the real thing. And so far away from the rest of the world.

During my ten-day stay, I didn't shop, sightsee or sleep more than an occasional nap. I lived on cafés con leche, little croissants called medialunas, chicken empanadas, and vino tinto, all on the run. At midnight I wrapped my feet and padded my toes before stuffing them into spike-heeled pointy-toed tango shoes, and then hobbled down the hall to the elevator. I suffered until blessed numbness set in an hour later. Then once the music began, I floated on air across the hard cement and tile floors of the tango halls. After one milonga closed, I went to another one, and when it closed, I had breakfast. Then I soaked my bloody feet in the huge lavender bathtub of my room at the Hotel Continental, throwing in as much salt as I could beg from the kitchen. I fell into bed each day at 6:00 a.m., smelling of men's cologne. I was deliriously happy.

I had to learn not to avert my eyes from a man's direct gaze if I wanted to dance at the Buenos Aires milongas. It wasn't easy for me at first to stare at a man from across the room, too forward for women in the U.S. It is considered rude in Argentina for a man to approach a woman's table without permission, and so a woman gives her permission silently with her eyes. Women have control. Often that's all that passes between a man and a woman before meeting on the dance floor, simply a look that says, let's dance together. After the man opens his arms and the woman walks into them, they hold each other wordlessly for a moment before beginning to dance.

The deep embrace, which is the norm in Buenos Aires, both seduced and frightened me. I was thrilled to be held in a close embrace and led strongly around the floor in a dance of beauty and passion; I could see how easy it would be to confuse the dancer with the dance.

It's possible that many American women like me are starving to give up control--at least for the time it takes to dance two or three tangos. And to be held so close that your breath combines and your legs tangle and you dance as one... well, that made the loneliness go away.

In Buenos Aires I learned that tango was music, a mystique, a way of life, a people, not only a dance. My skills improved after dancing twelve hours a day with strong leaders, and when I got back home to Los Angeles, I haunted the local milongas looking for a tango high. Instead of driving down the freeway every night to West L.A. and Rhinestones 'n' Rawhide, I drove to milongas all over the city.

I had already gleaned a lot from spending so much time at R & R—about codigos and dance etiquette, and leading and following, and now I knew it was to prepare me for the tango, the most profound and elegant of all social dances.

However, along with all of its other qualities, a tango can also be just a dance. Back home in the Los Angeles milongas, I reminded myself of that each time a man took me in his arms to dance, and before I went home, alone.

CHAPTER 22

MARIO EL MAGNIFICO

Dancing can reveal all the mystery that music conceals.

~ Charles Baudelaire

Mario Gonzalez, the Argentine tango star, was coming to Los Angeles on his first teaching tour to Southern California. He needed a place to stay--nine days' lodging in exchange for three hours of private lessons. I was a dancer; I moved. I had never met Mario although I had seen him in Buenos Aires when I was there two years ago, and of course everyone knew him from his role in "Tango: The Motion Picture." It was fun to share Chateau Rodney with visitors, and I was proud of where I lived. My apartment was comfortable and lovely, and it was always nice to have guests, such a change from living alone. During those happy years with Jack in our big house a mile away, we constantly entertained. And a tango luminary giving me free lessons in exchange? I didn't have to think about it.

Jeffrey the promoter picked up Mario at the airport and dropped him off at my apartment with his six pieces of expensive luggage, saying only, "Good luck!" with a wave as he strode back down the sidewalk to his car.

I had hoped we'd all sit around over iced tea and talk for a few minutes, easing me through the awkward moments of having an unknown man stay in my house. But Mario did it himself; he was charming and all smiles, remarking about seeing me around the milongas of Buenos Aires on my tango tour.

My apartment was walking distance to whatever one needed, a huge plus for visitors without a car. Part of the arrangement was for me to drive Mario to the milongas and his group classes, which was no problem as I would be going anyway. Women's offers to take him to the beach, Disneyland, on tours of L.A., were lining up and since I had to work most days, that took some of the pressure off.

After he got settled, we walked the neighborhood and he bought some takeout for lunch, insisting on washing the dishes after we ate. While he was checking his email on my computer, I played some tangos on the piano downstairs and he sang along. He had a good voice, and of course knew all the words. No one before had ever sung to the tangos I loved to play, and it made me feel whole, a real communion. I used to feel that way accompanying my kids on their horns during recitals and auditions, and it also reminded me of playing duets with my father so many years ago. For thirty minutes there at the piano I experienced my favorite thing—communication through music.

That night we went to the milonga where the L.A. tangueras went crazy over him. They circled him three deep and literally dragged him onto the dance floor. He appeared to be overwhelmed. He didn't dance with me until the very end, almost like a mercy dance. It was peculiar, as if he and I were

THE CHURCH OF TANGO

connected in an official way and that he "owed" me a dance. I suppose I did feel he should dance with me, his hostess. Later in the car he complained bitterly about the aggressive women. He was still wound up when we got home, and so I left him on the couch reading, and went to kiss his cheek goodnight in a "besito," but he grabbed me and kissed me strongly on the mouth. I wasn't particularly attracted to him—he wasn't a particularly attractive man— still I let him sleep in my room that night.

That day had been fun and I felt relaxed and happy. Playing house that way brought up old memories of contentment. It felt comfortable and natural to share my home and my bed with a congenial man, one with whom I had so much in common. It wasn't the sex I missed so much, it was the sleeping with someone. I hadn't planned on being seduced by Mario, just sharing my life with a tango master for nine days as a fun adventure. If that's the way it was going to be, well I was up for that too—a little mini-affair with a definite time limit, and lots of tango.

In the morning he cooked a large breakfast for us of eggs and ham, and insisted again on cleaning up the kitchen. We drove to the Valley where he was giving a workshop. He used me to demonstrate most of the time, and of course, like any other woman in that situation, I felt proud. It's not logical, it doesn't mean we are better dancers than anyone else or that the teacher especially likes us, it's just a thing that happens. Sometimes it's simply because the instructor doesn't know any of the other women and how well they dance.

The following day he gave me a private tango lesson. He had been teaching there in my studio and people had been coming and going all day long. My lesson was his last one, as I had been at work all day at the library.

After dancing with me for two hours, he changed the mood of the moves, and we finished the lesson in my bed. I had enjoyed our previous encounter, but it was fairly ordinary. Pleasant, but no big deal, and it certainly didn't last long. I was learning that he had deep insecurities, maybe being thrust to the top so quickly after that one movie was part of it, maybe his lack of confidence in his looks was another. He wasn't unattractive, but nothing special, with a pudgy body, which he always tried to hide by wearing baggy clothing, and a scruffy beard which perhaps he was also hiding behind.

He complained grimly about the dancers of Los Angeles, how bad they were, how aggressive and rude the women were, how he had no respect for them, as we drove to the milonga later. I chastised him by saying he should admire the people for paying him, for taking his workshops, for trying to improve their dancing. "The women take privates only to get to dance with me. I feel like a prostitute," he said.

"Then why not teach with a partner, like so many do?"

"Because then I would have to share the money!" he admitted.

When I tried to change the subject, he responded with dialogue quotes from "Tango: The Motion Picture," which I didn't recognize and he was piqued that he had to explain.

After the dance that night, a group of us, all Argentine except me, went to the only open restaurant to eat, a brightly lit coffee shop in Burbank. Mario sat at the head of the table and began to recite a long poem in Castellano. A very long poem. Everyone could speak English, but it was only Francisco who turned to me and translated the gist of it. It seemed funny, and people were laughing. Then Mario stood up and began another recitation or oration while our food arrived, and in total, he spoke for about an hour. There was no conversation or give and take, it was a monologue from start to finish, and after fifteen minutes even the Argentines were bored. I thought I would die from fatigue; it was three in the morning and I had worked all day.

"Francisco, would you mind bringing Mario home? I'm exhausted and I want to leave now and it looks like he is just getting going." Francisco lived in my neighborhood. I didn't mean to make any point by it, but Francisco and I used to date and he now put on an Argentine macho face of rage as if I were trying to make him jealous, "You want me to take him to your house? But who knows how late it will be?" he asked, softening.

"It doesn't matter—he has a key."

"He does?" He lifted his eyebrows.

"Sure, I can't have a houseguest I don't trust."

So I drove home alone, thankful to sink into my bed at 4 a.m. I was asleep when Mario got back, but he came into my room smelling strongly of liquor. He was all over me before I was even awake, and then stumbled back to his bed in the other room.

He kept the door to his room closed the next day. There was no more singing to my piano playing, no more, "I waited to eat with you so we could be together," no more washing the dishes, no more little gifts as in the past couple of days. No more playing house. We barely spoke. His manner had changed 180 degrees.

I drove him to teach his workshop, but was appalled at his sloppy appearance, so un-Argentinean. There were twice or three times as many women there as men, too bad, because the men really had more to learn. He was a good teacher, but arrogant. He approached tango intellectually, and told everyone they had to forget everything they already knew, that his way was the only right way. His English was fluent and he talked and talked about tango theory. The women salivated waiting for him to choose one of them to demonstrate with. He was finished with me.

Not only did he drink to excess, I was noticing he also used drugs. I knew he had diabetes and took drugs for that, but something else was going on. Maybe he needed all of that to cope with the adulation and stress of teaching, even though he should have been used to it. "Tango: The Motion Picture" had been out for several years by now.

On Saturday he was out all night, and when he came back, tried to force my locked bedroom door. He was obviously high on something.

Sunday morning I woke him up. "Mario, you are no longer welcome here. I refuse to be treated this way in my own home. When I get back from church, I want you and your six bags to be gone."

"Huh? But what about the workshop this afternoon? What's your problem?"

"I'm sure you will find a way to get there. And there are lots of good hotels. Here's the phone book—pick one." I threw it at him, hard.

We screamed at each other then like a married couple. It was bizarre to get wildly angry with someone I hardly knew and didn't care about. All the passion that should have been expressed on the dance floor erupted from us both in hot lava of hate. I yelled and cried as if it were the end of a long relationship, and he called me every filthy name he could think of in English and Castellano. I cried so much I got a sinus infection and was sick for a week.

I didn't go to any more of his classes, and I didn't see him again in L.A. I remained stunned and stupefied over the bad ending to what I had hoped would be an enjoyable nine days. It was just like dancing a tango—the beginning to the end of a relationship with all the associated emotions in a very short period of time.

The next day I saw Marisol in the courtyard. "Was that guy the famous tango dancer? He sure didn't look like one," she asked.

"I guess he acted like one. I had to kick him out, I feel terrible about it."

"You're kidding! You kicked out another guy? He was supposed to stay one more week, right? He did seem squirrely, though. Where did he go?"

"Oh Marisol, someplace else, thank goodness." I felt bad to have opened my home to a stranger, trusting him because he was well-known in the small tango world and to the organizer of the workshops, and that I had to ask him to leave. I strongly felt that for invited guests, "Mi casa es tu casa." And for him to have taken advantage of the situation and treated me without respect made me melancholy, especially after Olivier and the annulment of our too sad, too late, too desperate wedding. My guess was that Mario couldn't handle the stress of his fame, touring the U.S., and all the women clamoring for his attention.

In the years since my cancer and the shock of my relationship with Olivier turning out badly, I had much less patience for bullshit, bad treatment and disrespect. If it couldn't be my way, then they had to hit the highway. (Or I did.) Life was too short.

CHAPTER 23

TULIP TANGO

yes, set fire to frostbitten crops,
drag out forgotten fruit
to dance the flame-tango,
the smoke-gavotte,
to live after all....

~ Denise Levertov, "A Walk through the Notebooks."

It was a dark and stormy night at Schiphol Airport. Freezing cold, too. And far, far away from Los Angeles. For eight years since Jack's death I had been setting fire to frostbitten crops trying to "live, after all." Now I had come to Amsterdam in the middle of winter to dance the flame-tango.

I had reserved a room at the Hotel Fantasia on a canal in downtown Amsterdam, which was anything but a fantastic dream. Still it was clean and had a friendly and hospitable family of proprietors who lived on the ground floor. I climbed the wooden staircase to my long and narrow room with an iron cot and no hot water after eight at night. Located above the breakfast room, in the morning there would be a clattering breakfast buffet of sausage, cheese and strange dark breads.

I bought nuts and a cocktail in a little red windmill bottle at the reception desk for my Christmas Eve in Amsterdam dinner. I didn't feel alone or at all sorry for myself; on the contrary, as usual when I travel and am adventurous, I was exhilarated: a new country, a new language, new experiences and future memories. I called a cab to take me to midnight services after looking up churches (kerk) in the Yellow Pages. Built in 1392, the English Reformed Church was a perfect place to be on Christmas Eve. It was warm and welcoming inside, but the church filled up quickly and the overflow crowd stood under their black umbrellas in the rainy courtyard. How blessed I felt to be sitting in the snug, crowded church, and I sent my thanks up to Heaven as I waited in line to take Communion. My home church in Hollywood, which I loved, now had too many empty pews and the vacant seats next to me always held ghosts, even and especially on Christmas.

A friend of a friend's sister had married a wealthy jolly Dutchman, and through the kindness of strangers, I was invited to their house on Christmas Day. They picked me up at the hotel in their Mercedes and drove me around town first, so I saw the Reiksmuseum's facade, people lined up for a Christmas concert at the Concertgebouw, the front of Anne Frank's house, and the beautiful winter countryside full of fat cows on the way to the suburb where they lived.

After a merry family and friends' dinner and gift exchange, even with presents for me, they drove me to the train station where I caught the 9 p.m. train to Nijmegen, 160 kms from Amsterdam. My hosts must have thought I was crazy as I climbed into the cold train clutching my highheeled dancing shoes and waving goodbye.

But I was in search of tango. And I had heard about the famous all night tango marathons at El Corte, Eric Jorissen's celebrated school. Several European dancers passing through the Los Angeles milongas had mentioned Nijmegen as the best place in Europe to get a tango fix. When I had found out that there was also a tango festival in Amsterdam between the Christmas and New Year's marathons in Nijmegen, that cinched the deal. I was going to Holland for the holidays.

Anything was better than staying at home at this time of year. Since I had been alone, I learned to manage most celebrations, but Christmas without my family was just awful. Adam was up north with his cult family, and Jason, who had a difficult time at Christmas since Jack died, had plans with his girlfriend and her family. Besides, I've found that being alone in a strange place is fine and logical; but being alone in your home town is more difficult to rationalize. I'm not lonely in a place where I don't know anyone, where I am without expectations.

The first thing I saw when I got off the train at the Nijmegen station were acres of bicycles locked in racks reflecting the dim florescent lighting overhead. I had never seen so many bicycles, but it was so dark I couldn't see anything else. I wandered out into the black and deserted town and searched for the tango school. I was glad I had on wool pants under my short tango skirt, my hat, leather gloves, and heavy fur-lined parka.

I couldn't find enough light to read the location instructions I carried in my gloved hands. After patrons of several quiet bars pointed out directions, I found El Corte almost by chance as there was no sign, only a brass knocker on the door, which was partially blocked by rucksacks, sleeping bags, boots, parkas, and bicycle helmets.

As usual when I entered a tango space, I took a deep breath and paused to feel that flutter, that rush of anticipation fringed with fear. What will happen tonight? Who will I dance with? Would I go to Tango Heaven? I always knew that with dance, anything was possible.

El Corte was a modern building, still undergoing remodeling inside. It had a homey feel, with a loft and little walkways upstairs, and easy chairs and couches lounging around the several rooms. There was a kitchen with food and drink laid out. The wooden dance floor in the back had a high ceiling and dramatic lighting. The crowd was youthful, vibrant, beautiful, and could really dance. In Buenos Aires the talented young people I met had been preoccupied and focused on becoming professional dancers so they could leave Argentina to perform and teach abroad. In Europe the young generation danced because they enjoyed it.

I checked in with Eric Jorissen, a congenial, friendly and funny guy with a youthful demeanor himself, who has almost singlehandedly created Dutch tango mania. He handed out plastic pins of various designs and we were to find our "match" on a partner of the opposite sex. I never found the man wearing the pink and green angel wings like mine, but as soon as I changed into my tango shoes, I began dancing and almost never stopped.

I was one of only eight dancers coming from the U.S., and I didn't know the others as they were mostly from the east coast. The American dancers didn't invite me to dance that first night, but my partners included French, Swiss, Danish, and of course, Dutch dancers. It was such a pleasure to dance with the Dutch, as not only could they really dance in the close embrace style I loved and was used to from Buenos Aires and L.A., but unlike the Latinos, were very tall. Several men in Argentina had told me that they wanted to dance with me, but I was too tall! Because of dancing so close together, the size of your partner can make a big difference; the center of gravity is changed as well as your body position. It was a welcome challenge for me to dance with the Dutch.

It was freezing outside, but sultry, hot and smoky on the dance floor. The hundreds of dancers were almost all Europeans and smokers. Since the floor was so crowded it was a delicious challenge to do an intricate and emotional tango in just a few feet. There was a lot of pleasure for me to dance complicated moves in tiny ways, as that made the dance even more intimate. The steps were so small and hidden, that there was little to watch from the outside, and couples looked to be often in a tango trance.

The last train back to Amsterdam was at 7 a.m. but I couldn't tear myself away even though my feet were killing me. I figured I'd get back to the hotel somehow. And sure enough, at 9:30 that morning, as the cold sun peeked weakly up from the east, there was a place in a VW beetle for me with three girls from Paris driving back into town. Luckily there were still some dregs in the breakfast room at the hotel, and I made a couple of quick sandwiches and crashed in my room. Dancing so many hours in smoky El Corte had made me sick, and so I spent the day in my iron bunk taking antihistamines, resting up for the opening of the Amsterdam Tango Magia Festival the next day.

This three-day tango bash was spread out over Amsterdam in different studios and venues. Famous teachers from Buenos Aires were giving workshops, and there were milongas every night. At the festival registration, we were given bad maps of the various venues, but all of the streets looked the same, especially in the darkness that descended in mid-afternoon: canals, old Dutch row houses, bicycles. I couldn't tell one street from the other in this city lying completely below sea level. There was very little daylight at that time of the year, only from about 9:30 to 3:00, and I was even more confused in the dark. Winter is not the best time to sight-see in Northern Europe.

Somehow I found the appropriate place for the first class, but Pieter, a man I had met and danced with in Nijmegen, one of the few older than thirty and with grey hair, found me disoriented and put me on the back of his bicycle and rode me to the next workshop.

Being both "singles," we had been assigned unknown partners for the classes, but since mine from England didn't know his right foot from his left and I got tired of pointing out which was which, and Pieter's partner didn't show up, we decided to just dance together. Besides, we had enjoyed dancing together at Nijmegen and we kind of liked each other. Pieter had lived in Amsterdam all his life and was an artist, as his father was before him. He used to teach art, but now he essentially did nothing. He liked tango and he danced well, but he wasn't addicted or passionate about it. He invited me to lunch the next day, and I took a taxi to his house on the canal right in the heart of the city, close to the red light district.

He really did live in an ancient mansion, with several levels and stairs going in all directions, and cluttered dusty antiques and walls covered with paintings and objets d'art, and dead plants in dark corners. He microwaved something and we ate in the grimy glassed greenhouse kitchen, nothing at all like the elegant lunch chez Olivier so long ago. I could see he spent all his time in the front parlour in his worn chaise lounge easy chair. Everything important to him was within arm's reach: television, books and newspapers, his smoking supplies for his handmade sterling silver long handled pipe, and handrolled cigarettes. His veritable den, there was art on the walls, as well as scotch-taped memos and thumbtacked calendars and postcards. He had inherited the house, and sold off various parts of it over the years to provide himself with an income. Still, it was enormous, and I could only guess at its magnificence when he lived there as a child with his parents. I wanted to photograph some of the more bizarre appointments, but I was embarrassed to do so as it seemed rude.

Pieter was an excellent tango dancer. So we took the rest of the classes together, and explored Amsterdam. He took me to his favorite coffee houses on his bicycle, showed me the cafés where marijuana was served buffet-style, gave me a tour of the tattoo museum with a client spread-eagled on the icey floor having his full back decorated, and walked me past the prostitutes marketing their wares in the windows. I gawked as a customer left a storefront and shook hands with the fat, negligee-clad working girl in broad daylight, in front of mothers with babies and skateboarding kids, and tourists like me.

Pieter himself looked like a painting by Rembrandt. With crimson cheeks and cherry red lips, blue eyes, Ben Franklin glasses, fuzzy lambchop sideburns, longish gray hair, and of course that silver pipe, he was quintessential Dutch. A perennial bachelor, he was droll and eccentric and well-built (from all that bike riding and tango dancing) and a perfect companion for me. That we found each other was my Christmas present.

The first Amsterdam milonga was in Café de Kroon on Rembrands Plein, walking distance from my hotel. I invited my new friend—my Christmas hostess—but her husband didn't want to come so she brought her teenaged son. She had never danced tango before, but she enjoyed watching and some of my partners were gallant and invited her out on the floor for "walking" tangos. The milonga finished early (one a.m.), and most dancers went to another one in De Boksschool. But I changed my shoes and walked back to the hotel. Jet lag, fatigue and smoke were working on me, and I knew when I had to quit. It was raining, and I was astonished by all the people on bicycles holding umbrellas, as well as bags of groceries and sometimes bouquets of flowers as they rode, occasionally talking on cell phones as well. I welcomed Amsterdam's youthful energy, which was permissive and supportive at the same time. Old and historical, nevertheless the city had an avant-garde feeling of innovation that felt very exciting, even in the dark of deepest winter. I could only imagine what it was like in August.

The Roxy was the milonga venue the next night—a fabulous nineteenth-century wooden movie theater turned into a trendy nightclub. The Sexteto Canyengue played on the stage, and the teachers, Gustavo & Giselle-Anne and Esteban & Claudia, performed. Crammed with over 300 people, the energy, heat and smoke were palpable. I was glad I was with Pieter, because in that crowd with low lighting it would have been difficult for me to get a dance with strangers. As it was, the floor was so crowded we didn't dance all that much, but enjoyed the ambiance. Treacherously steep wooden stairs led up to the balcony where there was another bar, and people even danced up there between the jammed tables. Dancers climbed all over the stage and the three wooden bars to sit, to see the show, to light cigarettes. Colored lights bounced off the gray air. I was drunk on the smoke, music, and ever-replenished cocktail in my hand.

Gearing up for the New Year's two-day Marathon at Nijmegen, I decided to stay in a nearby hotel. It wasn't for me to sleep in a sleeping bag on the side of the dance floor. Let the Euro Kids do that.

So I made a reservation and told Pieter he was welcome to join me and be comfortable, and New Year's Eve we took the late train together to Nijmegen. The hotel was just a short walk from El Corte, and would be a convenient place to nap and shower. The dancing wouldn't stop for two days, and I wanted to miss as little as possible. And if Pieter and I were going to sleep together, I preferred it be in clean sheets and with hot water available in the bathroom.

Eric had more games planned for the marathon, keeping it alive and fun right to the end. He passed out blinking red heart clips that people fastened onto their shoes and shirts and hair, and then he turned out the lights and all we could see were dancing blinking hearts. The fabulous DJ kept surprising us with unusual pieces of music, and there was always something fresh to eat in the kitchen. With over 350 dancers from all over Europe, new partners were everywhere. But Pieter and I more often than not danced with each other. He told me he was "almost" in love with me.

Pieter wanted me to stay a few more days with him in Amsterdam, but I had plans to go to Copenhagen for three days to visit a Danish tango dancer I had met in L.A. at a milonga when he was passing through. How many times will

I be invited for a weekend in Copenhagen, especially when I'm already rather close by?

So Pieter took me to Schiphol, bought me a double CD of a Dutch tango singer, and kissed me goodbye. "I won't write," he said, "but I won't forget you.'

And off I went to Denmark, where Soren and I danced tango on the cold marble floor of Hamlet's castle. I was doing my best "to live after all."

When I returned home in a new year to Chateau Rodney and work at the library, the milonga at the Realtors' Hall in Burbank on Friday nights, it was the same routine, but I felt different, renewed. I felt great! Unfortunately, like always, it wasn't long until things changed.

CHAPTER 24

CHATELEINE NO MORE

We are confronted with insurmountable opportunities.

~ "Pogo," comic strip by Walt Kelly

The Chateau Rodney denizens didn't make a move toward any boxes before seriously discussing out in the courtyard how we could pool our resources to buy the building and live there forever. Even with several calculators and computers clicking, the numbers wouldn't crunch. Notwithstanding appeals to friends and family members to invest in what was for sure a sure thing, our building. If the new owner could evict us in order to triple the rent, what greater profits did the future hold? But we couldn't pull it off.

When the Chateau Rodney sold in 2001, we were all forced to go our separate ways: Steve and Cynthia rented another apartment close by but without charisma, Marisol, Derek and Joe bought houses in the Valley, Aimee went back to San Francisco, Ted moved to New York.

Because of the debility brought on by my cancer treatment, and the strenuous nature of working with the public in the library, I was able to take early retirement. It wasn't much, but I hoped I could live on that somewhere. I sure couldn't afford to live any more in the land of my birth now that I had to move from Chateau Rodney and my rent controlled apartment. Naturally I hated to leave my friends and Jason (Adam had gone up north to his group years ago). I hoped we could all stay in touch with email and chatting. The truth was that I didn't see all that much of my sons, living in L.A., which made me sad. I thought living far away where they couldn't come over for dinner or take me to lunch or even telephone me that often would make me feel better; lower my expectations and so have less disappointment.

I was angry that after thirty years of working for the library and my unfortunate health issues, I couldn't stay in Los Angeles living on my pension. I checked out rental options that were all more than half of my new low income, even renting a room in a house far out of town with a shared bath, not to mention car costs, so important in L.A.

But a part of me was also excited at being forced to move out of my comfort zone. I had wanted to live in France, I tried my best to do so, even attempting to prove that my grandfather was born in Ireland so that I could get an Irish passport. (Unfortunately, though I had always believed that he was, upon doing my research I learned he was born in New York.) When I was with Olivier I tried to get a job in Paris, but it was impossible because of not having the legal right to work. Even if we had married, I still couldn't work in France until two years afterward. But now I was looking forward to forging ahead in another foreign country.

I checked around for possibilities in places where I would have liked to live in the States, like Portland, Oregon, and Denver, Colorado—both with growing and exciting tango communities and lovely downtown areas. But apartment rents in those cities were almost as expensive as L.A. Nancy told me she read that Las Cruces, New Mexico, was the cheapest town in which to live in the U.S. Looking it up on the internet, I just couldn't imagine living there, a place where I knew no one, had no charm, and was only a possibility because it had a low cost of living index.

I decided to go to Mexico with Phoebe the cat where I hoped life would be easy, simple, rich with culture, and cheap. I read on the internet that San Miguel de Allende was an expat haven, and for that reason it was easier for Anglos to live there than in other more "Mexican" towns. Most businesses with services and products appealing to gringos spoke English, the tourist restaurants served disinfected food, the lectures and movies at the library were in English or had English subtitles, theater plays were in English. Since I knew no Spanish other than the bits and pieces I had picked up in Argentina, San Miguel seemed perfect.

When I browsed the webpages of San Miguel and saw the picturesque beauty of the photos, I made up my mind. Besides, Mexico was just across the border from California, although San Miguel was in the middle of the country and hard to get to. Still, just 2 ½ hours flying time from L.A. to the nearest airport in Leon. I could learn a new culture and language and still live in my own backyard, so to speak. And hopefully manage financially on my pension, impossible in Los Angeles.

My move was right before Christmas, which, looking back, seems to be a time of transition for me: Jack was diagnosed and operated on in November; I decided the first Christmas without him to go to Paris to study French; I moved to Paris on Christmas Eve with Olivier and no hair; last year I went to Amsterdam, and now I was moving to Mexico after six years of forging a new life in my hometown.

When I searched the internet for a San Miguel apartment, I looked for five things—low rent (the main reason for my move to Mexico), quiet, accepted Phoebe the cat, no more than a fifteen minute walk into town, and with a wood-burning fireplace.

I found one with everything but inexpensive rent, and I thought I'd try it for two months while looking for a more reasonably priced place. The fireplace was more problematic. Some landlords in my search told me via email that it's not P.C. to burn wood in San Miguel because there was so little of it and so their fireplaces were gas or they didn't have them at all. But I rationalized that a few logs from dead trees burned to help me keep my sanity was less damaging to the S.M.A. environment than a big American car driving around El Centro. Or a gringa run amok.

The Chateau had a giant combined yard sale on the front lawn. People recently arrived from other countries with money to spend gawked at and appraised the heirlooms I still had—my grandmother's Carnival glass and Fiestaware, the sterling silver I had collected since high school—I felt bitter and displaced. Why did I have to sell my heritage and flee to a third world country, while these recent arrivals got to build their new lives in the U.S. with my things? Dealing again with sales and cardboard boxes was more than I could bear. I finally sent everything important to auction this time, including my piano and my car, and the rest to the Salvation Army.

I finally sold on eBay the ivory wedding dress, lace pumps, and little veiled hat I had bought during my chemo to wear when Olivier and I married. Several neighbors ended up with what I considered souvenirs: handmade quilt by Jack's grandmother, an art nouveau tiled mahogany washstand, my mother's hand painted glass dishes.

It was tougher to give up being a dance critic with a free pair of house seats whenever a visiting dance company performed anywhere in Los Angeles or Orange County. It was fabulous, but most of all, I knew that my deeply considered reviews would always be published and read—not necessarily the case with my free-lance travel writing. But I was hired to write an on-line column, Mexico Diaries, as well as a column in the gringo newspaper in San Miguel. I had written book reviews and articles on assignment for Library Journal for many enjoyable years as part of my job.

It had been a difficult time, a traumatic time, these past three months since receiving the Notice to Vacate Premises at Chateau Rodney—the garage sales, eBay, packing and storing, saying goodbye to Los Angeles where I had been born, raised and lived all my life, bidding farewell to my job, friends, and the only family I still had, my two sons. It was sad that there was no one who remembered me as a child, no one who had known my parents. That's what happened when you are an only child, your father was an only child, your mother the youngest of her siblings who lived far away in other states. I had no cousins, aunts, uncles, nieces, nephews, or old family friends. I had my sons and the friends I had made as an adult, who I loved as family.

Now the farewells were déju vu of years before when I moved to Paris to marry Olivier, and another goodbye party seemed anticlimactic and overkill. So I went out to lunch or dinner with several friends during my packing period, and then Phoebe and I just planned to get on the plane to Mexico. However it was de riguer in Los Angeles Public Library to not slink away but to have a retirement party. Nancy organized one for me at the Echo Park Branch, and I danced a farewell tango with John from my tango class.

At Chateau Rodney we had a final glum and gloomy fiesta; our hearts weren't in celebrating the fact that Chateau Rodney was over and our family was going our separate ways after six years. The conversations veered to the past and what we would miss: the train whistle from far-away Glendale blowing through our dreams, the hand-pulled bell of the Old Catholic Church around the corner every evening at seven, the best croissants in L.A. at La Belle Époque, the carolers who came every year on the Saturday night before Christmas to sing around the lamp post in the courtyard. Even the balloon man felt deflated, and his creations that night lacked their usual joy. He should have used only black balloons.

None of us will ever forget, or be able to undo, the magic of Chateau Rodney in our lives. Living there, in that Shangri La or perhaps Brigadoon (no one parties with or even knows their neighbors in L.A.!) was just what I needed when I returned, beaten, from France and the relationship with Olivier. What we all needed. We went with the flow, and prospered. We were the "Las Felices" of the Los Feliz district of Los Angeles, and we knew it. Probably those parties are still going on there in the courtyard, even if only in our memories.

CHAPTER 25

CHRISTMAS MIRACLE IN MEXICO

Never ask God to give you anything;
ask Him to put you where things are.

~ Mexican proverb

"I made it! As so many have done before me, Phoebe the Cat and I arrived in San Miguel de Allende to begin a new life in the Colonial Highlands of old Mexico." So began my first newspaper column for Aténcion San Miguel on my expat experience. I did feel quite proud of myself for accomplishing this move on my own, and beginning a new life in a country where I couldn't speak the language. The truth was, it was exciting as well as challenging. I was the kind of person who felt better about a bad situation if I did something, anything; if I made a decision and went for it. Perhaps even a bad decision was better for me than to feel buffeted by winds and chance. I had been learning these past ten years since Jack's death that if I wanted something I had to go after it. Nothing wonderful would just fall in my lap.

Vicente was waiting for me with his taxi at the Leon airport holding a sign with my name as prearranged by my new landlady. The road to San Miguel was long and dark and

Vicente drove carefully, mindful of the topes (speed bumps) in the middle of seemingly nowhere, and the dead animals by the side of the road. The lights of San Miguel gleamed in the distant hills out of the shadowy countryside.

Soon we bumped along on the town's cobblestones, surrounded by adobe walls and a few old-fashioned colored Christmas lights, and strangely enough, Chinese lanterns. We passed a man in a sombrero and serape in a small plaza, and climbed up the hill and down a miniscule alley, where we stopped in front of a long wall at my new Mexican home. I carried Phoebe and Vicente brought in two suitcases. "But where are the purple bags?" I asked in panic. We searched the car uselessly, frantically.

My carry-on bags never made it out of the Leon Airport in Mexico—the bags where I put everything too important to be checked. I must have turned my attention to Phoebe, and poof, everything changed. And the timing couldn't have been more poignant--it was right before Christmas.

After getting Phoebe set up with her sandbox and dishes in the downstairs kitchen of our new place and trying to take in that I was now living alone in a foreign country, I searched endlessly through my two remaining bags for things that weren't there.

I went to bed but couldn't sleep. I only tossed and burned with worry about the loss of my irreplaceable belongings. I pictured someone picking up the bags, searching them for things to sell (my jewelry items only, probably), and tossing the rest out the window of a pickup truck on some dusty Mexican road. The image of my family photos blowing through the cactus just made me sick.

The next day my new landlady called the airport for me because as yet I had no Spanish. But the news was bad: no found purple bags. She counseled me to forget it and move on. Easy for her to say in the middle of her Texas mansion plunked down in a garden in a beautiful highland town in Colonial Mexico. Not only did she own her huge hacienda and my apartment, she also had built and rented out a casa and a casita all constructed in the same walled compound. And of course all four dwellings were full of her things. I only had a cat and four suitcases, and now the two most important bags were missing.

This new loss after so many recent losses in my life caused me to mourn for days. I went to lovely St Paul´s, the gringo Protestant church, and prayed to accept the inevitable.

The day of Christmas Eve, the town was full of people carrying baby Jesuses hurriedly through the streets on their way to all the Nativities where the Holy Child would later appear in ceremonies that included rocking Him in cradles of lace to lullabies. Poinsettias, or noche buenas, the largest I had ever seen, were everywhere—in fountains, in hanging baskets, lining stairways and courtyards. In the central Jardin, there was a living Nativity scene in the bandstand, with barnyard animals that children could pet. A tall young man encountered two nuns in their full white habits walking ahead of me on the sidewalk, and kissed their hands. I overheard him say, "Me encanta... me encanta," and the sisters smiled and laughed, not immune to the charms of a handsome man.

That night I went to a party given by a friend of a friend, and as seems to happen so often in San Miguel, in talking about a problem, help happens. I was learning that serendipity is the way here. At the party I met someone who was leaving the next day for New York from Leon, and she offered to inquire at the airport for me about my bags. I hadn't gone back myself because of the transportation difficulty—one hour, forty-five minute expensive taxi ride there and back—and my lack of hope in finding them.

I took the bus up to the supermercado on the hill and bought some new underwear and some makeup, although all of the shades were too dark for me. The bus was decorated with crucifixes and images of Our Lady of Guadalupe, and a boy dusted off the windows at major stops and then collected the fares in a plastic bucket. Gigante was like a surreal American supermarket, where things were kind of familiar, but upon close inspection were totally different. Open bins of sticky candies and pickles, and the smell of fish, strange looking plant things in the produce department, only frozen shrimp, ice cream and ice cubes in the freezer, guards with automatic weapons by the check stands.

The small supermarket in the center of town was more user-friendly, even though the funeral home next door featured a big stack of tiny white satin baby coffins in the display window.

I wore the same pair of earrings every day, but bought a beaded bracelet and necklace from an indigenous woman hawking them over her arm in a restaurant next to the Jardin.

At least I had Phoebe. I certainly would not have traded her for the missing bags, or anything else I didn't have.

For the first time in my life since the age of twelve, I didn't have to work. I had no job, or no one that expected me or medical treatments to show up for. Luckily I wrote travel articles and my column, but had no time clock to punch. Such a strange feeling of freedom, yet purposelessness. My daily mission became finding out where things were, and how to get things done in this new land. I quickly learned that each item on my "to do" list took at least four hours.

After five days, acceptance of the lost suitcases was growing. I figured this was just another lesson in how we don't need things, how we are here not to accumulate but to live and do. Looking at the poverty around me of the Mexican and indigenous peoples gave me a new perspective. I didn't really need so many pairs of earrings, how often did I look at those photos anyway, and if my friends wanted to contact me they had my address, even if I didn't have theirs. It would all work out, and I would be a better person for it.

I was sick and tired of loss, but wasn't this just another lesson in how to live on my own? We come with nothing, we leave with nothing; we can't take it with us, possessions are just a burden, etc. All the helpful clichés spun around in my head actually making me feel better.

Early Christmas morning the phone rang: "Cherie, your bags are here!" It was the lady from the party, calling from the airport on her way to New York.

I immediately called Vicente the taxi driver and woke him too. "I'll be right there!" He felt terrible and unnecessarily guilty about the loss of my luggage. "It was my responsibility, my job," he moaned in Spanish.

Twenty minutes later we were tearing along the empty Christmas morning road to Leon. At the airport we searched through the lost luggage and my bags weren't there, although there was a similar purple one and I thought probably that was the one my new friend saw.

Vicente also wanted to check in Customs up by the gate. When we approached, we saw my orphaned bags behind locked doors. There they sat, both of them, like my oldest friends in the world. Traveling unlocked with me on the plane, now they sported plastic security seals. I offered a tip, but the officials waved it away, smiling at the tearful reunion of a gringa and her stuff.

"Gracias, muchas gracias, Feliz Navidad!" I called, walking through the airport hugging my luggage.

Vicente and I laughed all the way back to San Miguel where, after cutting off the plastic locks, I found everything completely untouched.

Getting my things back was a miracle and the best Christmas present I ever received. Those five days without the security blanket of the cherished contents of my bags gave me perspective. I could have managed without them, I had been managing. It had not been the end of the world. I had even learned something about myself. Nevertheless because of the kindness of strangers and a miracle of good luck, I had a very Feliz Navidad in my new hometown, and an incredible Bienvenidos a Mexico.

Vicente invited me to his extended family's Christmas celebration that night. But that is another story of milagros, magical realism, and me in Mexico. (And another column for "Mexico Diaries!")

CHAPTER 26

HEART OF FIRE

I secretly understood: the primitive appeal of the hearth.
Television is—its irresistible charm—a fire.

~ John Updike

I needed a fireplace. I was alone, and a real fire was a living presence and company on solitary nights. I stared into it, adjusted the logs, watched the color of the flames, smelled the soul of the burning wood. While I was convalescing in the French countryside, the wood fire was my company. Gas logs are visual, not emotional warmth. Might as well put a fire video into the VCR as have a gas fire.

In the middle of January the cold snap hit San Miguel, with two days of icy rain. One small fireplace to heat a whole apartment on several levels when the temperature was below 35 F was like lighting a match. I knew people had lived for thousands of years without heat, but they perhaps became acclimatized. After only a couple of weeks in Mexico, I wasn't.

When I asked my landlady for a small electric heater to use in the bedroom and the bath, she refused on the basis of the electric bill, and had the gardener bring in more wood.

At the same time, the gas ran out and I had no hot water or cooking facilities. For the first time in my life, I had to shower and wash my hair in icy cold water during freezing weather. Even the much touted-on-the-internet microwave didn't get hot enough at night to warm anything, and I often had to run across the courtyard to her house to heat my dinner. The television reception at night also was nil, due to the higher use of electricity after dark.

As I wrote my column on living in Mexico, I sat with Phoebe on my lap, my feet on the hearth, and enjoyed the flames and embers for more than aesthetic and emotional reasons. I needed the fire to warm my cold body—as well as my soul. As for Phoebe, she soon discovered that the snug chimney was the ideal place for a nap—until I lit the logs and heard faint meows of panic from up above. I learned to check first, as being smoked out didn't dissuade her from her cozy den.

I quickly got back to basics in Mexico. Heaven can be cuddling under a quilt in front of a blazing fire with a cat in your lap. Heaven can be a hot dinner in the dead of winter, and hot water to bathe in. Heaven for me during my first two months in Mexico became simply the fact of being warm.

And another of my living requirements, the one about the fifteen-minute walk to town? I got that too, but didn't know coming back it was fifteen minutes straight up! I made the best of it because my body got into better shape and I could eat all the enchiladas and guacamole with impunity. Plus the hike kept me warm.

But I didn't like feeling—and being—so far away. Some days I just didn't have the energy to make the trip into town, and no one ever visited me high up on that hill. Even the taxis often refused to take me the last segment of the trip home at night, and let me out in the dark to navigate alone the steep and slippery river rocks of the alley where I lived. Lots of evenings I just stayed home.

I found out that even if I didn't take part in all the downtown action, I liked to think I could. After the two months of my lease were up, Phoebe and I moved down the hill to Calle Loreto, behind the church of the Oratorio—two minutes to everything. Now I enrolled full time in the Academia Hispano Americana to finally learn the Spanish my mother had urged me to take in high school instead of the French I insisted on. The intensive classes met every day from 8:30 a.m. until 6:00 p.m. in an old colonial mansion a few blocks down the street from my new apartment. There were classes in grammar, literature, conversation, folklore, and even cooking, all in Spanish. My favorite was history, as American schools didn't teach the history of our neighbor to the south. I knew more European history. I loved learning about the Aztecs and the many modern native tribes and languages, and a different point of view of the Conquistadores and Hérnan Cortez, and about the handsome Emperor Maximilian who was shot by a firing squad in the neighboring city of Queretero. When I arrived home every night I collapsed on the bed, too tired to eat.

Now in el centro, I was aware of the many town fiestas, and the constant festival of sound, some possibly charming—fireworks and church bells and crowing roosters at all hours of the night—or annoying, like the nonstop barking of the ubiquitous roofdogs and the chink chink bang of the construction that is always next door to wherever you are. The new apartment was convenient to the Academia and to the steep stony streets I trudged daily on errands, but had no fireplace. It was the end of February and very cold. I had noticed in Copenhagen in January last year when I visited Soren for a weekend of Danish tango after the festival in Amsterdam, that white candles were lit everywhere in homes and public places, filling the dark days with light and cheer. I went to the funeral parlor next to the supermarket and bought several creamy beeswax pillars that made the cold air in my apartment sparkle with living flames, and kept my spirit company—even if not my body warm.

CHAPTER 27

THE REAL ENCHILADA

Life is either a daring adventure or nothing.

~ Helen Keller

My birthday and spring arrived on the same day. Since I've always been a party girl, what better way to celebrate than to have a fiesta on the roof of my new apartment in the center of town! I didn't know many people yet after living in San Miguel for only three months, but I invited everyone in my Spanish classes at the Academia, local people I did business with, dance partners at the Agave Azul bar, and patrons at a Cuban art opening in the library.

What a great way to turn thirty-nine again! Music, food, dancing to my portable boom box under San Miguel's night sky, with rockets and fireworks exploding over the Parroquia! I was afraid someone with too much tequila might fall off the roof or down the spiral metal staircase, but no one did.

A Mexican man I had met at the art show at the Biblioteca was a big hit—bilingual, social, good dancer, amiable with everyone at the party. And so when he showed up at my door a few days later with a friend, I invited them in for a beer. We chatted for about an hour, I never left the room, and when they were gone, I noticed every centavo from my purse was missing (about $30 U.S.), my watch, and the worse insult of all, the Carlos Santana CD I had been playing!

Recently the English-language newspaper Aténcion San Miguel, the one I was writing a column for, published a front page article on the necessity of reporting crimes. I was going to chalk it up, but I was urged by many to report the theft to the authorities. Since I could identify a witness and a suspect, as well as give personal information about the possible perpetrators, I decided to follow that advice.

I grabbed my passport, dressed conservatively, and hailed a taxi. "El Ministerio Publico, por favor," I said. At this the taxista turned around in his seat and stared at me. And then we set off, driving out of town, and climbing up the steep back roads to the highway, passing the Gigante supermarket, the Cinema complex, and we kept going through the mesquite until we reached the prison. Several guards with automatic weapons were in front.

"Es el Ministerio Publico?" I confirmed with the driver. I really didn't want to get out of the car and go in there alone. But I made my way through the guardposts, and followed the pointing finger of a young guard to cross the yard under the gaze of the watchtower. I was so nervous, as if I had committed a crime. Were these guards really looking at me suspiciously?

I found the sign for Ministerio Publico, and spoke to a woman in uniform at a desk, but she barely gave me her attention.

"Alguin me robó," I said. Someone robbed me in my

home and I know who it was. His name is...

"Do you have a translator with you?"

"No, but I know the person and where he works. I want to make a report."

"Come back with an official translator." And she turned to speak to another person, dismissing me.

I persisted. "May I leave my name and address?"

"Translator," was her only response.

I went back outside, crossing the yard, and out onto the highway, just praying a taxi would come along soon. Being alone out there with the tumbleweeds in front of the prison along the traffic-free highway made me nervous. I started walking towards town, but being far from anyone made me more afraid than standing in front of the prison, where at least men in uniform were posted. So I waited, and soon I was glad to see a green taxi traveling out of town, but when I waved at him, he turned around.

Not knowing where to find a translator, or if there were requirements to function as one, I went back into town to the U.S. Consular agency for advice and assistance, where I was again frustrated. Even less interest was shown there. The Consular never even invited me into his office, we just spoke for one minute in the courtyard. "Be glad you didn't leave your name and address. There could be reprisals and revenge," he said. "Just forget about it, take care, and better luck next time."

I wrote a Letter to the Editor of the paper, and read with horror in more letters about the experiences of others. I was thankful that at least I wasn't shot, as one person was on his own rancho as he was trying to protect his well.

Since that first theft in my apartment, there were two more. But the worst part is that the thief returned three times to leave scary notes inside my closet, on the bed, in a portfolio high on a shelf, one note asking me to leave more money, that God would bless me if I did.

After my frustrating effort of skirting the guards with automatic weapons to try to do what I thought was right, I didn't try again to make another crime report. I did show the notes to my landlord (without any accusations), and amid lakes of tears, now I was the *mala persona* and the maid wouldn't clean my apartment anymore, which was probably just as well.

I changed the lock, but I lived with the drapes drawn, no longer feeling safe. One's home should feel like a sanctuary, even if it's a small rental apartment in a foreign country. In a way I was glad the original report was never taken, as then I would have feared reprisals. Being a woman alone and realizing how very vulnerable I was in Mexico was quite a shock. After traveling all over the world by myself and living in Los Angeles all my life, I never had been robbed.

I had followed the safety advice of knowing my neighbors, speaking some Spanish, wore my bag crossed over my chest, and all of the other things that were supposed to help me keep my hard-earned money, watches and costume jewelry. If I were wealthy you can bet I would have a security system, a security guard, a big dog, and a lawyer.

So when I predicted that the thief or thieves were aware they had carte blanche to victimize me and others with impunity, it unhappily proved to be true. And this in a town touted all over the media (AARP, Money Magazine) as one of the ten safest places in which to retire! It made sense, though, that if you were going to rob someone, it would be more worth your while and the risk to rob someone "rich." In every country where there was tremendous poverty, tourists were seen as wealthy. This attitude was perhaps even more prominent in San Miguel due to the high percentage of gringos whose presence had inflated the local economy. So sometimes foreigners were taken advantage of, shortchanged, charged a "gringo tax," pickpocketed, and like me, burgled at home. I already felt vulnerable; this proved I was.

CHAPTER 28

THE TITO TANGO

Listen, sister. I don't dance and I can't take time out now to learn.

~ John Wayne as Lt. 'Rusty' Ryan,
in "They Were Expendable" (1945)

Since I had to leave Mexico every few months for my visa, it was convenient to have all my cancer checkups in Los Angeles with my same doctors as well as see Jason and my friends. I always was able to find a few hours of work as a librarian substitute which I loved doing, and the pay, while not much, really helped. But during one such visit, after routine tests, my life was changed once more by mammogram results. Yes, I had cancer again.

I had two surgical lumpectomies in one week, and then returned to San Miguel de Allende to close up my apartment on Loreto, store my things and board Phoebe the cat. Then I returned to Los Angeles to begin therapy while staying with Jason in his bachelor pad. He gave me the bedroom and he slept on the couch. I promised to keep a low profile and to give him space when he had company.

I couldn't believe I had a whole new cancer, this time in my left breast. The doctor assured me that a new and different

THE CHURCH OF TANGO

one was preferable to a recurrence (!), and at least it was caught early, unlike the first one. So I wouldn't need chemotherapy this time.

I thought I wouldn't do chemo again. Once was enough. I hadn't taken the prescribed Tamoxifen years ago because of the side effects, and now I was wondering, and the doctor alluded that perhaps if I had been able to tolerate the drug, this second cancer never would have happened.

Why had I been taking all those expensive vitamins and food supplements in the intervening years only to have another cancer when I had none of the risk factors? Too late now. With cancer, nothing was sure. Once again, my body betrayed me. But unlike the first cancer seven years ago, I expected less of my body now. Because it had failed me once, I knew it could another time. Since the end of my last therapy, I hardly ever thought about it or the possibility of a recurrence. I certainly never ever gave a moment of time over to worrying about a new and different breast cancer. That's something I wouldn't have conceived of in a million years. Recurrence, OK, death, OK, colon cancer, OK—but breast cancer again? Hadn't I already gotten the tee shirt?

But Dr Hadassian was reassuring. "Your prognosis was pretty grim, that 24% survival figure. I hoped you'd make the five-year mark, and now look, it's been seven and that original cancer has not returned. So you have a new one, we'll just deal with it!"

He was right; I had had a 76% chance of dying before now, so indeed I was lucky and thankful.

Without an Olivier for support, or even my own place to live, I was determined to drag any pleasure I could out of life for the duration of my treatment. I was tenacious about having pleasure and fun whenever possible for the rest of my life. I went out to dance tango any time I wasn't too tired from my radiation therapy.

After my loneliness during the past year in Mexico, and before that in L.A. between Jack's death and my return from France, how could I turn handsome Tito away, even though the timing couldn't have been worse? Or maybe it couldn't have been better under the circumstances. I needed the distraction—and the endorphins—during the two months of treatments.

I was happy staying with Jason until we had a fight—another cancer was hard on him too, in addition to the prospect of my sharing his place for two months--then I slept on the couch at Nancy's. It was good to spend more time with her, but I really missed Jason. Maybe he was upset because I was seeing Tito, afraid perhaps of a repeat of the Olivier experience. I didn't understand how he could get so angry at me, especially during my cancer treatment, but if he didn't want me at his place for any reason, by golly I wasn't going to stay anywhere I wasn't welcome—just like I left Olivier's to go to Evian.

During the first week of my daily radiation at Cedars Sinai, Tito and I danced steamy tango nightly at several Los Angeles milongas. Age appropriate, he was very good-looking and an elegant dresser. His skin was golden and smooth, his body was lean and strong. An Argentine in the United States for two years, Tito knew no English. It would not have been feasible for him to have a relationship with someone without any Spanish, or so I thought. Thank goodness after my year of living in Mexico, my Spanish was passable. Unlike other Latino lovers I had experienced, who could express themselves with eloquent body language and a few choice words of English, Tito had no feel for language, not even his own. He mumbled and could not or would not remember to speak slowly to me. "Mas despacio, por favor," became my mantra.

None of this was important the night he took me home after the milonga. His kiss was expressive and powerful. He wanted more, and truthfully I could use some love. My poor body felt so abused from the two recent breast surgeries and the first week of radiation, and my soul and spirit felt beaten as well. I was being attacked from without and within and I had the scars to prove it. If someone I liked knew all this and liked me too, well, great. So when he insisted on going to a cheap hotel on Pico, I agreed.

The room was large but grim. I tried not to look too carefully. I only turned on the bathroom light. I also was hoping Tito wouldn't look too scrupulously at my body, with my scarred breasts and skin beginning to burn from the radiation. We enjoyed each other completely. He had a body that wouldn't quit, and there was lightening between us. He took a shower both before and after. His body was so clean and fragrant you could eat off of it. Even though it was late, or maybe because it was, the motel was very noisy. Lots of yelling and thumping and pounding and door slamming. Not too romantic, but quite sexy.

He telephoned me six times the next day, and generally every day. His cell phone was his security blanket; it had drips of dried paint on it from using it while he was working.

I agreed to go with him for tango practice at my friend's house. Blond Holly and I met at an L.A. salsa club a few years ago, and I had invited her to tango and we always sat together at the local milongas. She had quickly become addicted to tango, gave up her salsa dancing, and turned half of her house in Hollywood into a tango studio. She was a business woman with a talent agency, but now she seemed more interested and put more time into tango. Holly had been coaching Tito as he was anxious to learn to be a good dancer. He had never danced tango in Argentina, and now in the States he was hurrying to catch up. I enjoyed working with Tito and Holly. Not only was it a pleasure being in his arms, but I loved tango so much, even practicing with an almost beginner as he was.

When I danced I could forget how sick I was. Holly's boyfriend Ernesto, also an Argentine, would usually come to the twice-weekly practices, and she would make us all dinner. And then we would dance, usually with Tito and I staying overnight afterwards in her guest room.

He seemed always to be angry with me. My immune system was damaged from the radiation, and I got two infections, and sometimes I didn't feel up to having sex and only wanted to sleep with him. He was annoyed about that. He was annoyed that I didn't call him, or return his calls fast enough. I danced too much with other men. He was mad that I planned to return to Mexico when my treatments were over. He wanted me to go there to pick up everything and Phoebe the Cat, and move in with him in his single apartment in Glendale.

"Tito, we don't know each other very well yet. My life is in Mexico now. Let's wait and see what happens when I return to L.A. for my checkups in a few months. I'm not in the best position at the moment to make important decisions."

"I'm 52 years old, I don't want to be alone," he said.

"I want one woman and I love you. I can't wait a few months."

"I'll be back in six months."

"Six months? That's too long to wait."

"Well how long can you wait? Four months?"

"I'll wait two weeks while you pick up your things from Mexico."

He couldn't or wouldn't understand how I was the sick person, how much work it would be for me to do what he asked, how it was only me who was supposed to change my life--inconvenient, difficult, or not. Of course he couldn't visit me in San Miguel de Allende because he was illegal.

Throughout all this time, the first six weeks of my treatment, Tito never dropped by to see if I needed anything, brought me a little bloom or even asked me what the doctor said or how I was feeling. But then I was extra sensitive and after all, as a Latino, it of course was all about him, I knew that from the getgo.

I had been dating and searching for someone to love for years. I loved loving people, and now my "love circle" had shrunk right down to almost nobody but my two sons and a few L.A. best friends. There used to be so many people I loved in my daily world, and I missed them. It was difficult to even find a man I was attracted to. Tito and I had a tremendous physical connection, and despite myself, I cared for him. While the timing wasn't the greatest, the romantic attention of a gorgeous man when I was feeling so ugly, unattractive and old was the best medicine and a tonic for my mood and energy. I knew I got through my previous treatment because of Olivier. Cancer is not a one-person project.

When the end of my radiation was in sight, just another couple of weeks or so if my skin didn't burn too badly, Tito began to talk about marriage. I had told him at the start of our relationship that I didn't want to get married to anyone, and that I didn't have any money.

"That just proves how much I love you, because I prefer to marry you, even though you don't have a house, a car, a job, or money. But if you won't marry me, there are plenty of other women who will."

"What?"

"Mira, come look at my email," showing me his reams of messages from other women.

Apparently he had been keeping his options open during our relationship. He told me how many women called him every day, and couldn't understand why I didn't call him too. "But what do they call you about?" I asked.

He shrugged. "Nothing. To talk. I don't know, most of them don't speak Spanish." He told me about various inducements he had received from many women I was acquainted with. I knew that plenty of women found him appealing. He was usually the most handsome man at the milongas, if not the best dancer. If I hadn't been sick, and had been with him all the time at the tango dances, maybe he wouldn't have had so many women go crazy over him. I knew about invitations he had received to parties and dances from other women, and also those women who hired him to work for them and then came on to him. He always said he wasn't in the slightest attracted to them and I believed him.

Now when I read those women's emails, full of love and passion and invitation and proposals and offers, I was shocked.

One woman in particular kept calling him on his cell, often at three in the morning when he was with me or home alone, as he told me. Why didn't I answer it sometimes? At least at the milongas when his phone on our table rang at midnight and he was dancing, why didn't I pick it up?

He said he loved me. So I didn't care about all the people phoning him at all hours. He simply said they were loca, crazy, and I believed him. But when I saw those emails, I went a little crazy myself inside. My heart began pounding furiously in my chest, I could feel it through my skin and the throbbing scar on my breast.

I hadn't asked for this relationship, I wasn't looking to get involved with someone during my therapy; it was Tito who had made it happen. And now I had to go through all this anguish.

One proposal was from a wealthy woman in Redondo Beach. She had met him at a tango dance in Santa Barbara, and she had also traveled up to Los Angeles to dance at the Argentine Association, a milonga Tito never missed and one I never felt up to attending. My L.A. friends knew her because her body was malformed and twisted since birth. He had told me he had met her and that she was a good dancer despite her handicap but crazy and ugly, and couldn't speak a word of Spanish. Reading her bizarre emails, I saw that she was indeed strange. Since we were at Holly's house, I showed them to Holly, who started yelling too. And I was yelling in English and Spanish, and Tito got even angrier. Ernesto joined in and all four of us were screaming at the same time in two languages.

Holly was trying to explain the laws to him, that a marriage of convenience was illegal and they both could get into serious trouble, I was irate that he could say he "loved" me but was using this poor woman to get what he wanted while treating me like shit, Ernesto was trying to translate both English and Spanish but generally was just laughing about the whole situation, as he couldn't have cared less one way or another.

Tito said, "Since Cherie won't marry me, I am going to marry Jane. I am tired of being afraid of discovery and not having a good job or money. I want my papers. I've learned that in the United States everyone is out only for themselves, so I am going to help myself because Cherie won't help me."

He was correct about being afraid. He was afraid to drive his truck, and drove dangerously slow because if he got stopped for a ticket, he thought he would be sent back to Argentina. His whole life was built around his fear of deportation. There was a tango conference in Las Vegas to which he was invited free of charge by a L.A. teacher because they needed extra men, but he was afraid to cross the state line. I was supposed to marry him to "help" him?

When at last I knew from the doctors when I could leave Los Angeles to go back to Mexico, I bought my plane ticket. Tito told me he was going to marry the crazy woman the following week. She had set up a three-way phone conference with a translator and made him an offer he didn't want to refuse. He said he would have his papers in two months and then he could come to Mexico to visit me. I just rolled my eyes. "Claro, she will be thrilled to pay for your ticket," I said sarcastically.

Tito bragged that when he said Frog, she jumped; Holly and I both responded with, "Just wait until after the wedding. She will totally control you: where you go, what you do, who you dance with, and how high you jump when she says Frog, only you won't understand her because you can't communicate! She will control you financially, and by threatening to report you to Immigration."

No, I didn't contemplate for five minutes marrying him myself; I knew ours was not a permanent relationship. But emotions are not logical. Never having considered myself a jealous person, I had never been manipulated like this before either. Just to hear more details of the situation or to think about it made my heart pound, and yet I couldn't stand to not know as much as possible. Tito was silent on the subject, and ignored all of my questions. It wasn't just that he was going to get married to someone who was obsessed with him and who he couldn't stand; it was that he was going to do it two days before I left.

When I asked Tito to help me with my packing and to take me to the airport, he refused. I had had my chance, he said. Instead I packed up alone and it was Holly's boyfriend Ernesto who drove me to the airport.

The Saturday night before I left for Mexico, we sat together at the milonga. Tito wore a beautiful new cream-colored suit. I danced every dance with all my favorite partners because everyone knew I was leaving. I watched Tito sitting at the table, looking elegant and handsome and uneasy and stiff. He didn't dance often, and then it was generally only with Holly or me. He looked sad.

I could see how people get caught up in the romance of tango, how it's all illusion. He looked like a million dollars sitting there, but he was only a gigolo, for sale for the highest price. Women buy into the handsome milonguero fantasy, the lure of tango and the music and the passionate embrace, and often "buy" the man himself to continue the dream. But when the lights come up, the music stops and they go home together, the reality is that of an illegal handyman who can't pay his rent and can't speak enough English to order bacon and eggs at a coffee shop after two years of living in the United States. Of course, Tito had more going for him than most. He easily made the transition from ballroom to bedroom.

Holly and I invited Ernesto and Tito to an Argentine restaurant, Carlitos Gardel's on Melrose, for a "celebration" of his marriage, the end of my treatment, and my leaving--our last night together after so many over the past two months.

The four of us did nothing but argue and yell. I hated myself for the flood of sarcasm that poured from my lips, one nasty comment after another about weddings, marriage, love, about this being his bachelor party and I was the call girl who jumped out of the dulce de leche cake.

"Yeah, well, what's it worth to you for your bride not to know how you spent the night before the wedding, and with who?" said Holly.

Ernesto joined in. "Tito will be happy to perform his husbandly duties if he puts a bag over her head."

Tito said, "This whole bad situation is Cherie's fault because she won't marry me!"

I laughed bitterly.

Tito and I danced a tango in between the tables as the waiters and other diners paused to watch. Our last tango. I wore a low cut black lace dress with a scarf to hide my burned skin. We took photographs. He didn't thank me for the dinner.

We spent the night together at Holly's before he left for Redondo Beach in his truck filled with all his belongings. He was abandoning his apartment for the rest of the month, even though the rent was finally paid up with my help. He was Catholic, but she was Buddhist, and the wedding was to be in her penthouse apartment by the sea that day. He had pleaded with me to stay the night with him, but I had another infection. "Only to sleep," he said and I agreed, not wanting to forsake our last chance of lying together, but he forgot his promise, and got angry when I didn't dare take advantage of our final opportunity to make love.

The next morning he hardly spoke to me, getting his body as close to me as possible while getting dressed and silently motioning for me to button his shirtfront and cuffs and fasten his belt. "You are so handsome," I sighed, and he answered, "and may it serve me well."

He insisted on getting my phone number in Mexico and wanted to go to breakfast, but what was the point? I shrugged and walked alone to my rental car.

He emailed me a few times--the words to different tangos from the TodoTango website. He never called. I heard from Holly that he missed me but was more or less happy.

I returned to San Miguel de Allende, relieved and thankful to be on my own once again, and in my own bed, in my own apartment with Phoebe.

CHAPTER 29

CORPUS CHRISTI IN SAN MIGUEL

We ought to dance with rapture that we might be alive... and
part of the living, incarnate cosmos.

~ D.H. Lawrence

Back in San Miguel de Allende, with the little energy I had
after the treatment, the journey, the emotional affair with Tito,
I did my best with the errands, unpacking, organizing in the
new studio I had rented above an art gallery. I wasn't too busy
to notice the hanging of red and gold satin and velvet banners
from balconies along the main streets.

Thinking a weekend fiesta was in the making, I went
about my business. I was tired and almost ate a quesadilla
standing at the stove, which was my usual dinner fare in
Mexico. I decided to go out for a margarita instead and see if I
could find any of my friends, since I already was missing my
Los Angeles people—my neighbors at Chateau Rodney, my
old friends, and my sons, Tito too, if the truth be known.

Fragrant herbs covered the stony streets like a lawn. I
stood and stared at the cobblestones for a while as if the green
were a mirage in the dusk. My eyes just couldn't process what
they were seeing. The sweet perfume of the manzanilla and
mint made the dusty narrow roads transcendent.

Then I noticed large bouquets of crimson and gold flowers placed on the sidewalks outside several grand colonial doorways, openings that ordinarily are entrances to apartment buildings, shops, and restaurants.

Peering inside one such doorway, and not wishing to disturb the silent worshippers there, I saw a glorious altar, all in red, gold and white, with God the Father reaching down from a cloud. In another doorway-turned-chapel, was a tiny girl dressed as an angel sitting quietly on a white satin stool in front of an altar.

As my eyes got used to what to look for, I saw many altars, all different, in the center of town. There was an air of expectation, of emptiness, of waiting for the Host to arrive. With all the flowers, decorations and little live angels, still the altars were empty and lifeless as they waited.

Soon, naturally, a procession began to wend its way from the Parroquia and down the mint-and-flower-strewn streets. Stopping at every altar, the men carrying the litter with the Sacraments kneel, a priest takes it inside, and a prayer is read for that family, amplified by the speaker one man carries over his shoulder.

The people on the street often kneel too and make the sign of the cross and the men remove their hats. And then a rocket is shot off into the sky and explodes, either to scare away evil spirits or to alert God of what's going on here in San Miguel de Allende. Now the evanescent altars are brimming with life, at least for a few minutes before they begin to be dismantled as their purpose is fulfilled and life returns to normal.

The procession moves slowly forward along the proscribed route of crimson banners while a choir sings behind the accompanist who plays a Casio keyboard carried by four boys. Blessed fresh bread rolls, flowers, and herbs are given to the people at every altar. Sometimes the rocket frightens the roosting pigeons, which scatter, fluttering, as if they were released for effect on cue.

The small official procession is enlarged with hundreds of the faithful following behind, who respond to the liturgy with attentive Amens. The air is perfumed with incense and the streets become the church, the Body of Christ is literally brought to the people. It feels timeless, as if this yearly event has been reenacted for centuries, but it was only within the last decade that the Mexican government gave permission to observe this day with a public procession.

Certainly Corpus Christi was more than a town in Texas, it is a holy festival day nowhere more celebrated than in Mexico.

A few days later I went for a relaxing day to La Gruta, the mineral hot springs outside of town. When I got home I noticed a fleck of blood on the fresh surgical scar on my breast, and when I picked at it with my fingernail, blood began to pour from the incision spot. It was dark, thick, old blood, the color of burgundy wine. It had been three months since my surgery in Los Angeles, followed by the two months of radiation treatment; what the hell was this? Any time you see blood pouring from your body, you tend to panic.

The second cancer was now behind me, and aside from being exhausted from it all, I felt fine. While I hadn't actually leapt back into climbing the hilly narrow streets of San Miguel with my usual speed (I'm a fast walker), I tried to return to my old routine as soon as possible. Springtime was gorgeous there, with sunny crisp weather and many gringo activities like art shows and writing workshops and theatrical performances, and lots of Canadian snowbirds.

There was no oncologist in San Miguel de Allende, so I went to the only doctor I knew, the dermatologist. She recommended someone in Celaya, the next largest town nearby. So, packing my bra with paper towels, off I went on the bus, which I learned to call the "Burro Bus" as it stopped at every burro crossing and for every crate of chickens in the dusty desert. The trip of 45 kilometers took three hours, but at least little boys with tuneless guitars kept me entertained by hopping aboard to strum some notes for a few centavos.

I talked positively to myself: Gee, what an interesting experience, really culturally educational, look at all the plastic trash bags shining on the mesquite trees as if they were flowers. In Celaya I took a taxi from the bus station to the hospital Guadelupana in the center of town.

Dr. Sergio Iniguez Llano's office was clean and cool. His receptionist/assistant (a young girl in jeans) welcomed me and told me to undress, giving me a blue paper blouse. I liked Dr. Llano. His diplomas said he had studied in New York and Tokyo, he spoke a little English, he had gentle soft hands as he examined me, and was very good looking. He withdrew three hypodermics of blood, and had me walk downstairs to the lab with one of them to check for errant cancer cells. He said there was lots more blood, but he couldn't extract so much at once and I needed to return several more times. He shot me with antibiotics, and actually used the scary word, "metastasis."

The long ride back on the burro bus wasn't so interesting, as now I tried to think of what I'd do if there were more cancer. I didn't want to make this six hour round trip to Celaya very often, neither did I want to go back to L.A. and sleep on Nancy's couch again so soon. I wanted to stay home in Mexico, with my things and Phoebe the cat. After the terrible trauma of sleeping on couches and as a long-term unwanted guest in Paris, I knew I needed my own space to be happy. But I had already learned that what I wanted and what happened weren't necessarily the same.

When I went back to Celaya the following week, the lab test was back and no cancer cells had been found in that tube of blood. But my breast was still so full of it that Dr Llano ran out of hypodermics and had to borrow some more from another office. He said that it was probably from the radiation, although he admitted that in Mexico they have little experience with adjuvant cancer therapy, as the women normally wait until the last minute to see a doctor about a breast lump out of fear or pride. And then there's nothing to do but remove the whole breast. End of treatment. He said there wasn't even a radiation machine in Celaya, and he had very little experience with the side effects.

I noticed that Mariane, the assistant, had kept my paper blouse, and so I put the same one back on. Disposables really aren't in poor countries.

When my Mexican friend who I had met at her mail forwarding business, heard of my trouble and the painful jostling in the burro bus, the next time I went to Celaya she took time off from her job and drove me. It took forty minutes by car. And I wasn't alone. I enjoyed it. We had lunch afterwards.

Eventually all the blood was removed and my breast healed. And I forgot about it. But not about the kindness of my friend. I was so much less a stranger in a strange land after that.

CHAPTER 30

DANCING DOWN THE AISLE

I would believe only in a God that knows how to dance.

~ Friedrich Nietzsche

I danced down the aisle of Saint Paul's Anglican Church in San Miguel twice a month, carrying my cross. Like most people, I always had a cross to bear, except for that perfect time of my marriage. And now I had a literal one. I was a Crucifer. The cross I carried was very beautiful, made of stained glass and Tiffany jewels.

And I did dance with it, the processional step-pause of a wedding, and always in time to the hymn being sung. I wore a white alb, usually my San Miguel cocktail huaraches and a small ruby and silver cross made by a local jeweler.

It was such a blessing for me to serve in this way. I felt proud and humble and thankful. The Mexican people were accustomed to physically participating in their religion on a daily basis, unlike the Protestant gringo and Northern European. I felt so envious of all the processions and the full-blown, emotional festivals I witnessed in Mexico, longing to be a part of them. In my own quiet gringa way I built altars in my apartment, and lately in the business offices of my busy Mexican friends. I was always in the streets for the processions on feast days, and went alone at midnight to the Panteón on Day of the Dead, wishing I could join a family celebration on the grave of a loved one. What an exquisite and moving tradition to have a special day to honor one's dead with remembrances and fiestas.

It was so healthy for the living to remember their loved ones and to contemplate their own mortality in a personal way. Jack's grave in France was a plot leased for only twenty more years, my mother was buried in an old graveyard in downtown Los Angeles, my father's burial place was in the Valley with my grandfather's, and my grandmother's ashes were scattered at sea before she allowed me or my children to be notified of her death. No one visited, and certainly no one partied on their graves, bringing their favorite foods and drink and flowers to lure their spirits back for that night, unless it was a Mexican family's overflow. Now I learned in San Miguel how to lure their spirits back to me once a year with a simple trail of marigolds.

Here in Mexico religion was everywhere, and I was thankful I had one too. Maybe I wasn't a Catholic, but it didn't matter. I understood the sufferings of Jesus, and his mother, Our Lady of Sorrows. I prayed to the same God, and the complicated legends and stories that Mexicans grew up with now enriched my faith too. I was moved to touch the old beloved images the people kissed and adored even though it was not in my culture as a Lutheran, but I was blessed just the same. All the thousands of saints and the Hosts of Heaven and the Orishas of Cuba looked after me too, and I was thankful I at last found out about them.

The previous Easter season I made the midnight pilgrimage from Atononilco, a beautiful old church (called the Sistine Chapel of Mexico) in a village 17 km from San Miguel, an annual tradition for over 250 years--carrying a sacred image to San Miguel for the Easter season. About 6,000 people walk along in silence behind El Senor de la Columna in the light of torches, with rockets going off at the head of the procession to announce our arrival. Then at six on Sunday morning, when we entered San Miguel, thousands more people lined the decorated streets in welcome, offering the pilgrims hot food and drink. We stopped there to unveil the images, and then continued on to the church of San Juan de Dios, walking through the mint and manzanilla and elaborate designs in colored sawdust covering the cobblestones, our footsteps scattering in an instant the beautiful patterns incorporating Catholic and indigenous designs that took all the previous day and night to make.

My personal cross has been heavy at times, with all the illness, death and loss of the past decade. But I always had help in carrying it, and now to lead the procession to worship in a beautiful little church in Mexico was my blessing.

CHAPTER 31

SEARCHING FOR SALSA MEXICANA

To watch us dance is to hear our hearts speak.

~ Hopi Indian Saying

Unfortunately the best salsa in San Miguel de Allende was the kind you put on your tacos. Mexicans loved to dance but didn't want to be tied down to formal patterns or anything too complicated that would spoil the fun. In San Miguel there was music everywhere--mariachi bands waiting for gigs hanging out in the Jardin, strolling Renaissance groups in velvet breeches playing mandolins in the streets, jazz at the gringo bars, loud rock bands from Mexico City in the teen hangouts, disco music at gay bars, and the brain-and-body numbing bass thumping out of souped up pickups, especially in front of my apartment at three in the morning. If people listened, they were not dancing but tossing back beer, tequila shots, and on Wednesday nights at Harry Bissett's, martinis. These folks had other things on their minds than dancing. Most of the social dancing was done at weddings.

In the Gringolandia that was San Miguel, the salsa scene was anything but spicy. The few bands had no venue, as there was no real dance club, no space to bust out of, just ones you needed to get out of. Mama Mia's had what I thought of as a mosh pit for a dance floor, and at the Agave Azul bar, you had to dance in the hallway. La Cava de la Princessa's uneven rocky floor was passé.

There are many more places to dance in Guanajuato [a 90 minute drive] because it was a university town, but the road was so dangerous at night with speeding drunk drivers and dead animals that I didn't want to go, even on the bus.

I also went to a tango class but we were three women and one man. Dance teachers and many of the students came and went from San Miguel so often for whatever reasons, that a consistency was impossible. People were never quite sure when or if there would be a next class. The teachers came and went, the students came and went, and the locals were left with cumbia and ranchera music with which they were quite happy, but didn't satisfy me in large doses. I had hoped if all else failed I could join a folkloric group, as some years ago I danced professionally as a soloist with AVAZ International Dance Theater in Los Angeles. But there was no folklore group in San Miguel other than culture classes for children and teenagers. I would look silly as the only tall, older, and gringa member of any such group even if they would have me. On festival days the groups of Indian Conchero dancers came from all over Mexico to dance a sacred marathon in front of the Parroquia, but as fascinating as it was to watch, there was no way they would let me be one of them.

Then I discovered danzón! I had seen the movie and took a workshop in L.A., but I thought danzón was a boring old folks' dance like the box step rumba. But this dance had a style and pattern all of it's own, requiring attention to detail and to the music. Far from being simple, danzón had more than 26 patterns to mix and match to some really ear-catching music. It was the most formal and elegant of the Latin dances, even including tango. Danzón began in Cuba, then moved to Merida, Veracruz, and Mexico City, with each place having its own technique. I learned the Mexico City style, which had the most complicated patterns. In Cuba, it was the first rhythmic couples' dance in which men and women could dance face to face and close together, and for that reason became wildly popular. Later, with sexy son and salsa, it became a senior citizens' favorite. Cuban danzón has fewer patterns but more body contact, which made perfect Cuban sense.

On top of encountering danzón, I found flamenco, or flamenco found me—a relationship made in heaven. Daily classes helped me keep my general dance technique up as well as my sanity. Flamenco came naturally to me for some strange reason, (maybe because as one tango teacher observed, I sometimes was like a "wild horse") and I had little trouble learning the compas, palmas, zapatoados, falda, golpes, although I never wanted to take up a pair of castanets. Flamenco was danced alone, too, no partner needed.

Where I lived in San Miguel—my third apartment in twenty months—were five live music clubs on my one block of Mesones between Hernandez Macias and Hildago. Jazz at Tio Lucas, jazz/rock/pop/latin/accordion at Agave Azul, rock at Panchos y Lefty's, not sure what at Los Angelitos, and a very loud guy on guitar directly across the street at El Caporal seven nights a week. It was tough, especially in May the hottest month of the year, because I had only two windows, and they opened directly on the street. I always left my rooftop door open for air, and the sound came down the stairs. I heard different bands all through the night and I knew their repertoire so well I knew which song came next. This was compounded by band concerts and the police drum and bugle corps practice in the Jardin. The gringo bars, Tio Lucas and Agave Azul, shut down at a decent hour, but the three others went until dawn. And then I had the drunks under my windows. Usually it was just before sunup that I heard the clop clop on the cobblestones of the pair of mounted police, a comforting sound but too late to tone down the noise.

As in Paris there were laws in Mexico about hours and decibels and disturbing the peace, but the mordita (payoff) ruled. I went twice to see the mayor at the Presidencia, and I called the Ecologia so many times at three and four in the morning they just said, "Oh, you again."

Still I loved the apartment. Somehow it reminded me of Olivier's in Paris, with its floor to ceiling red draperies over the tall french windows. It was the first of the three Mexican places I rented that felt like home. Only one room, but it was a big space, filled with interesting old furniture and warm reds and golds. I hung my grandma's Navajo blanket behind the bed like a headboard. The bathroom was miniscule and the small water heater on the roof only allowed two minute showers. There was no heat so I boiled water on the stove.

The private roof terrace was all-important although I rarely went up there, and Phoebe was afraid to be there alone. It was psychological—I had light and air up above along with the possibility of ascending to enjoy the gorgeous view if I chose. When I moved in I fantasized about romantic evenings

THE CHURCH OF TANGO

on the roof and even paid a handyman to install a light. I took the bus to Queretero and bought a plastic lounge chair at Costco's but I never lounged in it. I didn't have guests up there for more than a quick look-see. I imagined putting in more potted plants, maybe even a clay pot fireplace or at least a barbeque, but these things didn't work for me alone. When I went up there to sit or to look at the stars, I said, OK, now what? I don't like the sun and I don't smoke.

One morning when I opened my drapes, a hot air balloon floated in the sky above the colonial building across the street. There was often a parade of some sort below my windows; certainly I knew I was in for a long night when the man set up his tray-table convenience store on the corner and began his song of "Aguas, dulces, chicles, cigarros!"

San Miguel's theater, the Teatro Angela Peralta, was only a couple of doors down, next to the Agave Azul bar. How I loved scooting there in half a minute to see whatever program was playing, especially in August during the Chamber Music Festival, which had the likes of the Tokyo String Quartet, the Fine Arts Quartet, the Yings. At the Peralta I saw a fabulous Guelaguetza performance from Oaxaca, incredible flamenco show from Leon, and I performed tango and a solo belly dance myself as well as flamenco on that stage's splintery floor on several occasions.

Unlike the other foreigners, I never sat in the Jardin, a beautiful place to relax, read, remember. There were too many loud-talking gringos and too many Mexicans waiting for an opportunity to take advantage of them. At night when there were festivals and entertainment, I was uncomfortable going alone due to the Mexican attitude that a woman out by herself at night was only looking for a man and the Mexican men want to oblige. The reputation of gringa women didn't help. It was true that many dressed revealingly, many to show off expensive boob jobs, and were easy sexual targets (not necessarily the same woman, but we all looked alike). Because many women on vacation came to San Miguel for a "fling," I was determined not to enforce the stereotype of being easy, and avoided opportunities for encounters. Many times I wanted to wander around incognito, just another person about her business.

What bothered me the most of all was that, besides flamenco classes and the occasional danzón, there was no dance for me in San Miguel. Still, I was happy with my cat, computer and books in a place that was beautiful and culturally profound. What was missing was the human communion and affection that the tango can provide.

Like in France, I loved the custom of the besito, little cheek kisses for everyone, and that even men hug each other in greeting. But without family, or a romance, or tango, that was the only physical contact I had. That was one reason why old ladies "doctor"—as my grandmother called it—so much; human beings naturally crave human touch. Unfortunately I couldn't say that psychological and emotional communion were any better or more frequent, but those were even more difficult wherever you may be. I was an affectionate person, in my element with a loving husband and children to care for. Where did all that loving affection go when suddenly all the beloveds were gone? Like Jason said, I was a people person with no people.

I really missed the tango, and a couple of times I made the four-hour bus ride on my own to Mexico City and stayed overnight in a hotel just to attend a Saturday night milonga at a Argentinian restaurant. But for what that cost me, and the fact that as a tourist I needed to leave the country every three months anyway, I just planned to go to Buenos Aires for a couple of weeks every so often. It was incredibly cheap after their economic crisis of December 2001, when there were five Argentine presidents in a matter of weeks, and the peso, which had been fixed to the dollar, devalued. All of a sudden the dollar was worth three times as much. And the tango was priceless.

Chapter 32

The Beauty

Like an invisible thread, envy entangles the dancers around the dance floor and the tables. Deadly sin that everybody commits. The ones in the back envy the ones in the front row. Those who come with their partner envy the loners, the loners envy the couples. The young envy the experience, the old ones, the freshness. Those who work early envy those who can stay up late, the unemployed envy those who have a job. The foreigners envy the portenos, and the locals envy those who come to steal the girls or the milongueros...

~ Sonia Abadi, El Tangauta, Feb 2001

Santiago was like a cat, a beautiful proud tom that lived off his wits and body. Women were drawn to him, well, like cats in heat. The first time I saw him was in La Confiteria Ideal when I was visiting Buenos Aires from Mexico.

In the afternoon, the tables in the Confiteria Ideal--an elegant Belle Époque hall of marble and mirrors on the second floor above a bakery and tearoom--are littered with the cell phones of businessmen and of housewives, and with frosty ice buckets chilling bottles of sparkling sidra, the Argentine apple-cider champagne. People went there after work, or instead of work, or just to watch the action. The ballroom was beautiful, the service was terrible, there may or may not be running water in the ladies' room. But only the dancing mattered.

Santiago was sitting among the men, and I sat at a little table with the women on the other side of the room, as was the custom. When I caught his eye, he nodded his head in the way of the Argentine tango code, and we met on the dance floor. From a distance it appeared he was no more than 29 or 30, but up close I could see the crinkles at his eyes and the vertical lines on his handsome face. He was exotically dark, having Indian blood in a land which had all but obliterated its indigenous people, and had thick curly black hair that he wore long, down his back, tied at the nape of his neck. Unlike the older milongueros who haunted the salons in three-piece woolen suits, Santiago wore tight black jeans and a thin open shirt, the better to show his muscled body.

When I pointed him out to Cristina, my "maven" and B&B hostess for my two week tango vacation, she called him *The Beauty* and shook her head with a smile. "I never trust a man who is too good looking," she said. Small and voluptuous, Cristina had an infectious smile and a bubbling sense of humor and love of life. Affectionate and caring, she also had her standards as well as fiery relationships with friends, family, guests, and lovers. If she loved you, she really loved you. If she didn't, she was always polite. Most of all, she was fun and funny, and time spent with her was a pleasure.

Sitting with Cristina at the milongas and listening to her wise and witty comments about the men, women, and how everyone danced and behaved, captivated me. After six years of being a tango guide and hostess to dancers from around the world, she had perspective. She had seen it all, night after night in the milongas. Being a psychologist all her life hadn't hurt either. She often had to be a Mother Teresa to people whose world had turned upside down in the tango scene of Buenos Aires. She knew how to cheer people up with a party, with jokes and laughter, and with compassion. Every night spent at the milongas with Cristina was another tale to tell.

On the dance floor, The Beauty and I just nodded wordlessly, and he enclosed me in the tango's intimate embrace. I wrapped my left arm around his neck, and he held me tightly with his right, as if he were hugging me affectionately to his heart. My face was in his long fragrant hair. He smelled like the incense that took my breath away in church. I closed my eyes. He led me and I followed and we created something new together with the music.

Between songs we discovered that neither of us spoke the other's language, but nevertheless we were communicating. He was one of those people who seemed to have sparks flying off them, who drew everyone's attention when they walked into a room or moved on the dance floor. And the sparks from his eyes shot into my soul.

After the tanda I was thankful for the custom of the man escorting the woman back to her table because I was dizzy and faint and disoriented. I sat down clumsily, and he left me to go back to his table among the men. Usually it was best to simply leave the milonga after a dancing high, to go with the glow, I had learned. But today I yearned for more; I didn't abandon hope until the last note of the evening was played, but we didn't dance together again that night.

When I saw him next at Club Gricel, a throng of tourists, probably American from the look of them in their bright colors and poufy blond hair, surrounded him. The women smiled and laughed with open mouths and gave him all their attention, the sole man--unmistakably the cock of the chicken yard.

When he asked me to dance, he performed for his flock. I didn't mind. I was glad he had left his henhouse and picked me. Later he approached the table where I was sitting with Cristina and spoke quietly to her in Castellano. "He wants you to go home with him," she said, turning to me.

"OK." I looked at him.

"Oh for Pete's sake, be a little hard to get! These guys enjoy working for it. Seduction is part of the fun."

"Too late." I smiled.

He nodded seriously, grabbed his backpack, and waited by the door while I said goodnight to Cristina. I didn't care if people saw us leave together, socially forbidden in the codigos of the milonga.

It was four in the morning, and there was no one on the streets. A balmy breeze puffed at the fallen leaves and through my hair and we walked on the cobblestones with shadows of trees from the full moon, me in my spike heeled tango shoes. It was very pleasant after the smoky salon. Even though my feet hurt after so much dancing, I could have walked with him forever.

He paused and looked at me. "el amor?" He pointed to me, then to him.

"Si," I said, and he kissed me. We walked some more in the quiet street.

"Hotel?" he said.

I said, "Si."

Then after another block, "No dinero," patting his pockets and shrugging.

I stopped. "Mi no dinero," I said, reluctantly showing

him my wallet with ten pesos in it, wishing one of us had whatever it took for a hotel room.

Then he asked, "Tarjeta de credito?"

No neon sign announced the small hotel, a *transitorio*, where couples paid by the hour. Santiago seemed to have found it by radar. I lurked in the corner of the dark reception area, conscious of my short black dress and fishnet stockings. Santiago dealt with the desk clerk who was sealed behind a window, probably bullet proof, I thought.

The room at the top of the stairs was all mirrors and pink satin, and very clean. The bathroom was also the shower, and I turned on the faucet and watched the water spray over everything, including the toilet and sink. There was a squeegee in the corner for drying the tiled floor. While he took a shower, I quickly got undressed and wrapped myself in my black-fringed shawl.

The headboard of the bed was like the cockpit of a jet plane: controls for everything—different lighting combinations and effects, radio, the TV. I wanted the light out so he wouldn't see me and my body scarred from cancer, age and childbearing, but at the height of his acrobatic zeal he flicked the switch to turn it on. I needn't have worried about him scrutinizing my body, because he had eyes only for himself in the mirrors around and over the bed. We were interrupted by a knock on the door by the reception clerk. I hadn't signed the credit card slip, and it was passed through a sliding window making opening the door in flagrant delecto unnecessary.

Afterwards he was tender and gentle, and explained

in simple Spanish about his family, his many brothers and sisters, the death of his mother when he was fourteen, and now how tango was his life and family. It was amazing that I could understand him. And before he slept he had me repeat in Spanish that I was his woman. "Cherie de Santiago." How ridiculous, I thought while enjoying the conceit, and the sound. He had a throaty way of saying his name that was like a purr.

I couldn't sleep. By the window's moonlight I marveled at his halo of jet black hair on the white pillow and his strong profile with his striking Indian nose. He had a tattoo on his upper arm of a heart with, he had told me, the names of his parents—Juan y Maria. So physically different from Olivier, from Jack. How odd at this time in my life! And why was he naked next to me? He was wildly attracted to me? Hardly. I was easy? Maybe. He wanted something else I had? Money? But I had made sure he understood I had no money, hadn't I?

I heard the clop clop of the junk man's horse-drawn wagon, and later the laughter and bustle of children waiting under our window for the school bus in the dark morning as I lay there feeling Santiago breathe and my heart beat.

I may have been "Santiago's woman" but I wasn't the only one. In fact, after our one night at the *transitorio*, he was more or less "bought" by another American woman, making me think of Tito and his green card marriage. At least that's the way I explained it to myself, as Santiago no longer danced with me in the tango salons. He danced only with a large middle-aged woman who couldn't dance very well, but probably paid for more than one night in a transitorio. And they sat together, something not done unless a man and a woman are a "couple." So I figured he just went to a higher bidder, even though I hadn't bid, or he had me and therefore lost interest. Or maybe he had really understood that I wasn't rich, living as I did in a rental apartment in Mexico.

When my two weeks were over and I was returning to San Miguel, we said goodbye on the stairs of La Ideal. He said excitedly that he would be leaving himself to go to the U.S., traveling to teach tango in Atlanta, the fat lady's hometown. He wanted my phone number and my email address, and I imagined him with an index file of American cities and the women he had met who lived in them.

⁘

The tango opens your heart and makes you take risks. The passion of the music, the dance of close embrace and tangled legs and pheromones, as well as the Latin culture from which tango springs, made feelings and normally suppressed emotions and longings stream from the eyes and ooze from the pores. I was an emotional person with an open heart, but the tango made me even more vulnerable. And since all of the cancer and loss in my life lately, why not take risks? Why not live for today and take chances?

I saw the female tango tourist from the north looking around at the many good dancers who were eying her as fresh meat, making her feel like she's died and already in heaven, especially if she's "older." It happened to me too. But I was learning that under the façade of pure tango love and dedication lurked ambition, desperation, insecurity, frustration, poverty, buying and selling of favors and dancing, jealousy, backstabbing, deceit, lying, manipulation, self-centeredness, and greed for both money and attention. For many dancers in Argentina, like Santiago, their bodies, their dance skills, and talent for charm were all that they owned in this world and they were going to use them however they could. So much like Tito, who had it all but the great dancing.

———

Santiago took his index of women contacts with him to the States when he went to Atlanta. He emailed me regularly and a couple of times even telephoned me in Mexico. Doris, "La Gorda," had built him a dance studio in the basement of her large home in the suburbs, gave him access to her computer, telephone, car, and I supposed, to her. But then he said that she was "loca," had thrown him out one late night to sleep outside in the cold. Why do men accuse women of being insane when they don't put up with bad treatment? He was saved by another Atlanta woman who took him in. Santiago's gripe was that Doris was in love with him, whereas for him it had all been a business arrangement from the getgo: so many hours of private lessons in exchange for room and board, similar in a way to my experience with Mario in Los Angeles.

"But Santiago, did you sleep with her?" I asked. My Spanish was improving and so was his English.

"Of course I slept with her! So what? It was only business."

His two-month tourist visa was almost up. Was I going to be in Buenos Aires when he returned?

"I am moving there permanently next year," I said, something he found so hard to believe. "San Miguel is getting too expensive, and I need the tango. Maybe I should have moved to Buenos Aires in the first place instead of Mexico. I'll be going again in a few months to look for an apartment."

Hasta pronto, we said to each other over the phone.

When I arrived in Buenos Aires a few months later, dancing at the Confiteria Ideal felt like I had never left. Certainly the building never changed, including the hole in the dance floor's pink stone surface near a marble pillar and the gorgeous cage elevator that never worked. I saw many of my favorite dance partners, both the host and the DJ remembered me warmly, or at least acted like they did, and Cristina was at a table waiting for me. There were the Barbies sitting over in the corner, the two women with long hair and miniskirts who looked like teenagers from the back, and old ladies with bad plastic surgery from the front.

I only had eyes for Santiago. But a previous flirtation of mine was there as well, a milonguero who also made his living teaching tango to foreign women. He had invited me to dinner once and bought me roses off the street, but then the next day at the milonga asked me for a loan. That got old. So we didn't dance anymore. Too bad, as he was fun to dance with, except when he was showing off for his friends at tables on the dance floor, leading moves to exhibit his partner's derriere.

It's a tough call: if they want to have sex with you and invite you to "coffee" and you refuse, they no longer will invite you to dance. If you agree to sleep with them, then they no longer invite you to dance after the conquest and it's over. You can't win.

Santiago and I fell into the habit of having dinner after

the milonga at inexpensive places, primarily El Tenedor Libre, a chain of cheap Chinese-owned buffets. Yes, sure, I paid.

Santiago's only source of income was from teaching. And actually he was an incredible teacher. He had marvelous technique and was able to pass it along. There was no fooling around or flirting when he taught, he was seriously all business. Tango wasn't fun or a means to an end, it was his life.

But he kept instructing me at the milongas. Once he starting teaching me, he couldn't stop. He would get angry if I slipped on a slippery floor. "Look at me! Do I slip? No, and you must not either!" My dancing became personal to him, and it wasn't the same as before. Instead of dancing in the moment and enjoying the music and the connection, I worried about my little mistakes upsetting him.

He took me to his hotel one night, sneaking me into the huge old building of several floors that once, maybe a hundred years ago, had been grand and graceful. Now it was a flophouse, a *conventillo*. The bathroom was down the hall, and there also was a community kitchen of sorts on each floor. His room was tiny, neat and windowless, and full of his two unpacked suitcases from his recent return from Atlanta. We had to be quiet, because he would have had to pay for me to be in there with him, or maybe it even wasn't allowed.

He asked me if I wanted to sleep there with him, but I couldn't wait to leave. I was afraid I would have to use the bathroom, and I didn't want to even see it. He helped me to find a taxi but not before saying, "You know, it's silly for you to pay for a room and for me to pay for this one, which as you can see, isn't nice at all. Why don't we stay together someplace?"

"We can't, you know, at Cristina's. She doesn't allow

that. But there's a tango house near by that I know about. Maybe that's a possibility."

So we moved, he and I, to the Tango House. We had a nice room, with a bathroom right next door. There was a communal kitchen downstairs, and best of all, a studio where he could teach and we could practice. Cristina told the manager, a crazy old witch of a woman, that Santiago was a visiting tango professor and I was his girlfriend. Otherwise there might be problems about a local milonguero and a tourist staying together.

Santiago had said he was a good cook and enjoyed it, so we invited Cristina for dinner, and he prepared a marvelous traditional country meal while I just watched and then did the dishes after Cristina left. I liked playing house. It felt comfortable and familiar.

During the two weeks there, some nights Santiago stayed out watching football with his friends as he said, or doing whatever, it didn't bother me. He didn't smoke, drink or use drugs and he didn't mind using condoms. He took care of his body because he knew that was all he had. When we ate together, I bought the food, but it was inexpensive and didn't add up to much.

I bought my own ticket into the milongas, and he got in for free. Several of the milongas paid him and other popular milongueros to come and dance with the women who didn't dance a lot, similar to the policy of cruise ships. So he and I couldn't dance too much together, which was fine because I enjoyed dancing with many men, although he was my favorite. Of course there was the chemistry, but also his high level of skill. Despite my not enjoying his picking apart my dancing in public, I was improving.

He drove me to the airport for my Aero Mexico flight. The car was his pride and joy, the only thing he owned besides his dancing shoes. He looked sad to say goodbye. "Email me," he said, "not every day, but maybe three times a week, OK?"

CHAPTER 33

TANGO HOTLINE: (718) EL TANGO

You tango with the devil all night long,
rise with the sun and sing the Lord's song.
You're on your way to an early grave
Keep dancing with that poison
and you'll find your way

~ the sister of a young heroin addict

My name is Cherie and I have a Tango Addiction. It could be worse--nicotine, alcohol, cocaine, gambling, heroin. But still I spend time and money I don't have chasing down a possible high anywhere in the world. When it's good, it's so very good that I want more, I need it again. I want it now! And if I don't get it, withdrawal begins to set in and I get desperate for my next fix

But where is it? A certain partner, certain music, dance hall, vibe, ambiance, mood? How to get it again? Maybe in Mexico City this weekend. Maybe in New York. Maybe in Buenos Aires. And, off I go, credit card receipts trailing behind me. After all, endorphins are chemical, a drug. It's easier to buy a fix of illegal substances than to go to Tango Heaven. It's elusive, ephemeral, often just ahead, I know it, the next time, place, partner, tanda will give me the tango high I need and want.

Before my next trip to Argentina, I invited Santiago by email to stay with me during my five days in a Buenos Aires hotel with last fall's arrangement in mind. I thought he would enjoy getting out of his flophouse and into a decent hotel, and the packaged five nights in a convenient hotel and airfare cost less than my usual plane ticket. Last fall it had been his idea to move together; as he put it, why should we each pay for a room when we can room together?

He offered to come to the airport to meet me, but I wasn't surprised he didn't. Soon after I checked in to the hotel in the Congreso district, he showed up and registered. He had an excuse about his sick father or his car or something. He had streaked his gorgeous black curls, and from a distance his hair almost looked gray. He patted his small potbelly saying, "Too many hamburguesas y cappuccinos en los estadosunidos!"

We immediately went to La Ideal; I only excavated my tango shoes from my luggage and left everything else in a tangle. It was Sunday afternoon and I couldn't wait to see Cristina, my other tango friends, and the milongueros. At La Ideal, Cristina observed that Santiago was acting like an "hysteric." He ran around the room from woman to woman, and the only way I knew he was with me was his cell phone staking a claim on our red tablecloth. Cristina knew what the situation was between us, and that I was crazy about him, but she was also a porteña who understood beautiful milongueros like Santiago.

The next two days were the same, but worse. Monday after the milonga at Canning, he didn't return to the hotel or leave a message. I soon had enough. Tuesday at Viejo Correo, I went up to where he was sitting at a table full of young pretty girls and inquired very loudly, "Cuando venis al hotel a buscar tus cosas?"

He said, "Que?" as I stared at the shirt I had brought him from Mexico.

I repeated even louder, "When will you come to the hotel and get your things?"

"Hablamos manana!" he almost shouted at me, and turned to the stunning girl next to him, dismissing me.

When he showed up at the hotel the next day, I presented him with a list of words and phrases from the Spanish dictionary to describe why I was unhappy: *grosero, tonto, imbecile, solamente un rato agradable*. He asked, astounded, where I had learned them. *Se acabo*, I said. It's over. I left to meet Cristina to look at some rental apartments for my future big move, after agreeing he could take a shower in the hotel room before clearing out. I wanted to remain friendly. So it hadn't worked out to stay together for whatever reason of his, still we could be pleasant about it.

But when I returned later to the room, there were more of his clothes there, like a tomcat marking his territory. I threw them in a plastic bag, even the gifts I had brought him from Mexico, and gave them to the maid.

That night I was sitting alone in El Beso when he flounced in with an older French woman who, coincidentally or not, sat next to me on the banquette near the bar. After parking her at my side and giving me a kiss on the cheek, Santiago went off to work the crowded room and I started a conversation with Simone in French.

"Oh you take lessons from Santiago? Yes? And you take him to dinner as well? That's nice. Oh, I have to leave now, would you be so kind as to give him a message for me? Please tell him that I threw his things at the hotel into the trash." Simone stared at me. I went to Lo de Celia to dance with the *viejos*.

When I returned to the hotel around 3 a.m., I had his name removed from the registration. "Senor Perez se fue."

The next day, my last before going back to Mexico, he showed up late at El Arranque. Cristina said he was looking at me, but I never looked at him in the tango code of invitation. Finally when my friends were leaving for dinner, he walked over and greeted everyone stiffly. And then to me, "Quieres bailar?" A milonguero never approaches a woman's table to invite her to dance.

"No," I said coldly, grabbing my street shoes and coat, and stalking to the lobby to wait for Cristina and the others. I was worn out, emotional, hurt and hungry. I couldn't breathe anymore, or watch Santiago dance with another. I knew what kind of man he was, but still I hadn't expected this, even though of course I should have. Six months ago when we stayed together for two weeks, it had worked out. I had no reason to think it wouldn't work this time for only five days. I didn't understand why he even agreed to stay in the hotel with me in the first place. I couldn't put up with his rejection for more than two days. The woman in Atlanta took two months!

I wanted to help him as it was true he was a gifted teacher and dancer, of course I wanted to have fun with him. Most importantly, I wanted to dance with him. Why it didn't happen goes into the mystery box with all the other questions I stuffed in there since Jack's death. Maybe I made a mistake not to dance with Santiago at the end? Couldn't we have forgotten all of the rubbish and had a flash of fun?

I learned one thing: a man can be handsome, he can be nice and a good person, or he can be a good dancer. You can have any two out of the three, but never all. I guess Santiago was a handsome good dancer, and that had to be enough. Maybe it was enough to be The Beauty.

CHAPTER 34

TANGO MAGIC IN OAXACA

If we are always arriving and departing,
it is also true that we are eternally anchored.
One's destination is never a place
but rather a new way of looking at things.

~ Henry Miller

I wanted to see more of the country I lived in before I left Mexico to live in Buenos Aires. A change from always flying south to Argentina, I travelled twelve hours south on the bus to Oaxaca, a state capital city that was as breathtaking as the travel magazines say it is.

Imagine a large leafy square with fountains and huge trees, surrounded on four sides by the colorful arcades of ancient colonial buildings. Imagine the kiss of a chocolate scented breeze on your skin. Imagine a concert band playing classical music under the trees, while elderly couples rise casually from their benches to dance an elegant and sophisticated *danzón*.

Oaxaca was the second poorest state in Mexico but one of the richest in tradition, cuisine, culture, and natural beauty. Although a large city, it felt small and accessible, and it seemed I could walk anywhere I wanted to go. That night I went to El Sagrario, a three story café-restaurant-pizzeria-nightclub close to the zócalo. Two live bands alternated, so there was constant music but little dancing until a group of three young men from Veracruz arrived. Luckily they sat near me and once the band found their salsa groove, the three of them kept me dancing.

Saturday night I attended an outdoor chamber music concert by the Mozart String Sextet with the full moon rising behind the elegantly rococo Santo Domingo church as a backdrop. I attended Mass on Sunday morning and marveled at the dazzling gold leaf inside, such a contrast to the gorgeous green limestone exterior.

After church, I headed back to the zócalo for the noon concert of the Oaxaca State Concert Band. Today the band set up under the large trees instead of in the art nouveau fantasy bandstand, the plaza's centerpiece. The many folding chairs were already full of Sunday-best elegant locals, European tourists, gringos, indigenous folk in their ethnic clothes, children and babies and grandmothers, teens and the many shoeshine men, who kept on working during the 90 minute concert on customers happy to listen as they sat in comfortable padded chairs on wheels. The eclectic program included "Bolero," "Granada," and "Deep in the Heart of Texas."

A little boy selling Chicles stopped in his tracks, enthralled, a foot away from the first trombone player and appeared hypnotized for the length of the piece. Another Chicles vendor, a middle-aged indigenous woman, stopped working the crowd when the band struck up the *Pineapple Dance* from the *Gueleguetza* folklore, and clapped joyously with the music. Everyone jumped to their feet and sang the final piece, *Oaxaca Linda*, the state anthem, with love and pride. I had never seen such a magical blending of an audience, although I knew music did that.

I was so filled with joy that after the concert I couldn't do anything but relish it. And so took a seat at one of the many zócalo cafes, ordered a cup of chocolate, and watched the parade going by my table.

Good natured vendors of small wooden toys plied their products to us sitting ducks at the outdoor cafes. To the contrary of being bothered by the vendors, it was a pleasure to sit in that lovely spot and have the wares come to me. And if I refused (how many chicken paddles can you use?), the sellers continued on with a smile.

A beautiful dark and slender young woman balanced a huge basket of red roses on her head as she crossed in front of me like a dancer. A candlelight peace vigil was making a presence in these last days before the Iraqi war. A mandolin quintet, with claves, was singing everyone's favorite songs for a price.

The many colossal balloon clusters of invisible vendors seemed like eerie, silent witnesses to the life in the plaza. They bobbed, pulsed, breathed, appearing to me like living plastic and mylar beings of great wisdom. Zócalo life could come and go, but the balloons saw it all and weren't telling.

As I walked back to the hotel, I glanced into the courtyard of an ancient building and saw dancers moving together without music. Stopping I looked harder because what they were doing reminded me of tango. A closer look told me it was tango, or was supposed to be.

Drawn inside like a magnet, I entered and asked a seated woman if this was a rehearsal for a dance performance. No, it seemed this was a tango class! "Well," I said, "I am a tourist here, but I am a tango dancer."

The class came to a sudden halt, and I was swept toward the teacher, a skinny toothless old man. Someone punched play on the boombox, and nothing would do but the old man and I had to dance a tango together for the camcorder! After what was a very painful experience because he hadn't a clue how to dance but must have picked up some choreography from Rudolf Valentino movies, they turned the video camera on me and asked me to dance solo! I danced a solo tango which is now preserved, on video in Oaxaca, Mexico. I talked to some of the students, danced with young Alejandro and exchanged email addresses, and I sashayed on my way feeling like a movie star.

The next morning at an internet ice cream store, I ordered two scoops of ices—Zapotec Dreams and Tamarindo with Chile—to refresh me as I pounded out descriptive email to my friends who had never had the good fortune to visit Oaxaca. And then I ordered one more flavor—Mescal! I hoped there would be time before going to the bus station to have another meal on the zócalo—out of the seven types of mole, I only had tried two.

I loved Mexico and wished I could afford to visit all its nooks and crannies. I had never even gone to any of the famous beaches. I knew in my heart of hearts that I couldn't continue to live there for various reasons, but mostly because of the high prices and no tango. Still, it was a culture rich in history, music, folklore, mythology, religion that I could identify with. And full of surprises; who knew I would find tango in, of all places, Oaxaca?

CHAPTER 35

LEAVING SAN MIGUEL

That terrible ache and nostalgia for home
when home is gone, and this isn't it.
And the sun so white like an onion.
And who the hell thought of placing a city here
with no large body of water anyway!
In less than three hours we could be at the border,
but where's the border to the past, I ask you, where?

~ Sandra Cisneros, Caramelo

In the evening flocks of grackles wrote V's against the mango sky. The setting sun shone through the dusty dome windows of Las Monjas one block west, and I could see the towers of five more colonial churches from my rooftop. Almost every day beneath the windows of my apartment passed processions of pilgrims, celebrants, or mourners. The Virgin sat on the back of a pickup truck or thirty schoolchildren carried an enormous Mexican flag or peppy tuba bands and old men, hats in hand, walked behind a hearse.

Even so, after two years in Mexico I had overdosed on the traditional fiestas that used to enchant me. As someone who enjoyed the Latin passion in the culture of France, I couldn't find the same energetic *joie de vivre* in Mexico. Mexican *allegre* was not a moving, pulsing force, but comfort and relaxation—abundant good food, bright and happy music, flowing beer and tequila, family togetherness and church. The sole ecstasy I witnessed was in the many fervent religious activities. I missed the zest and energy on the street and in the music that I found so compelling elsewhere.

I liked greeting friends and acquaintances whenever I stepped out my door, yet the population was transitory, and new friends were hard to keep, often leaving after a short stay to return home to Canada or the United States. Real relationships had little time to develop. I became leery of caring for a new friend because I knew they would soon leave. Sometimes it was painful to live alone in one of the most romantically beautiful places on earth, looking out my windows at the indigo sky and the lights of the Churrigueresque skyline twinkling below.

My circle of friends had changed. My favorite bar had closed, and even before that I stopped going out in the evening. Long ago I had given up on dating anyone. Pablo—my personal trainer—was the only man I saw in San Miguel, and that of course was a secret.

Over the past couple of years, I found that without realizing it, I was drinking too much, too often, as a way to be with people. Lately I might go to Harry Bissett's on Martini Night, and after two Cosmos and a bowl of guacamole, the smoke and the cackling Texas laughter would drive me around the corner and home to solitude.

In my cozy studio, I read, worked on the computer, wrote articles and emails to the world "out there," and watched Mexican TV. The folks I counted on were the women in my cancer support group, my friends at church, the group of writers who met at my house weekly, my fellow flamenco students, as well as the two or three friends I made at the bars when I first arrived. I had some Mexican friends by now, too, yet somehow there was always a gap between us which wasn't a problem of language. I guess it was cultural differences, although I hated to think that was possible between people who cared about one another.

There were several different social groups in San Miguel, and I didn't fit into any of them: the cocktail party circuit; the landed house builders, remodelers and decorators who had inexhaustible discussions on whether to paint the sala saffron or aubergine; the old hippies in beads; the Texas Junior League women with perfectly streaked blond hair and chunky silver jewelry active in charity fundraisers; the gringa owners of boutiques and businesses; the newly reinvented artists; and of course the Mexicans who had little time to spare away from their work and families.

Where I felt empowered, at my best, and at home was with dancers. In San Miguel I had searched out dance in studios, schools, clubs, theaters, parties, and discos. I tried Sweat Your Prayers on Sunday mornings, folk dance at the Bellas Artes, contact improvisation, Mexican folklorico, salsa in classes and clubs, and took the bus to Mexico City in search of tango, the immigrant's dance. More than a hundred years ago in Buenos Aires, the lonely porteño, far from his loved ones in Europe, was drawn to the connection and nostalgia of tango. In Mexico one's family is large and ubiquitous, and people live for the moment. Unlike me, the Mexican has no need to search for a family in a milonga, and Mexican tango is almost an oxymoron.

Finally it was flamenco that saved me. And after a student flamenco recital in which I did a solo belly dance, opportunities presented themselves to teach La Danse Orientale, to perform, to collaborate creatively with the flamenco teacher and musicians. But then what? I couldn't afford to keep going in the financial hole every month and manufacturing my own artistic outlets. I knew I couldn't live forever in the expensive Brigadoon Gringolandia that was San Miguel. If I did, I'd soon be one of the crones sitting in doorways with knarled hands outstretched to passing tourists.

Much of the Happy Hour conversations now centered on how the town had changed and how expensive it had become. I had done my best to live within my budget, moving three times to cheaper and smaller San Miguel apartments, nevertheless from the beginning it had been an impossible dream in the most costly place to live in Mexico. I had increasingly gone into my savings, and soon they would be gone.

San Miguel de Allende had been my home throughout three icy winters when I wore dance tights 24/7 and my electric throw over my shoulders on a long extension cord. And during two hot and breathless springs, when dusty winds covered the town filling my lungs with desert sand, bus exhaust, and dried dog and burro dung. The weather-perfect months in between I reveled in the afternoon rains, the ideal temperature, and the dazzling colors of the bougainvillea-bejeweled colonial architecture. Now the pleasure I found in San Miguel was no longer enough especially when the cost was so high, and not for the rest of my life.

I learned a lot in Mexico, I had made friends, I loved my apartment and the beauty of the town, where, like at Chateau Rodney, I heard church bells and train whistles calling me to places far away. Incredible luck and serendipity had given me the key to a Bosendorfer concert grand piano at the Hotel Aldea, which I played three or four times a week. However now it was time to move on—to someplace where the cost of living was less, where there was symphony and ballet and art museums, to someplace where I could dance more than solos. I yearned for the embrace of tango.

After more than a decade of searching, it looked like my future would be in other places, other hemispheres. I missed Los Angeles and the United States, and if wishes could make it so, I would still be living with my family in our house in Los Feliz under the Hollywood Sign. I had twice paddled in the River Styx, and now I was blessed with the chance of forging another life. I would have designed a different path for myself, but my life unfolded without consulting me.

Once again I bid farewell to a mixed group of folks who had welcomed this stranger into their lives. I was going to miss the man selling cigarettes and sodas on the corner, the flower seller who made the rounds of all the bars and restaurants every night, the girl who practiced her cello while working in the gallery below my apartment. I was worn-out from the partings and leave-takings of the last twelve years. But in Mexico, where nothing was as it seemed, "manana" didn't mean tomorrow, and "Adios!" was not goodbye.

CHAPTER 36

THE MEXICO CITY TERMINAL

The journey is the reward

~ Taoist saying

It's a long four-hour trip from the highlands of San Miguel de Allende to the airport in Mexico City. Once we hit the auto route Phoebe's meowing from the carrier in the back seat ceased for the long haul. I felt nostalgic to leave Mexico where I had lived for more than two years. So very many things here I loved, but the truth was, it was time to move on. I was finally going to live in Argentina, which after their economic crisis of 2001, was one of the cheapest places on earth to live as well as being the cradle of tango.

Jorge let me out in front of the hotel and drove the van into the underground parking garage. My flight was first thing in the morning so we had to do it this way, overnight. I sneaked Phoebe into the hotel under my raincoat, and Jorge brought up my carryon and his gym bag, leaving my two suitcases and four big boxes in the van. As when I moved to San Miguel de Allende from Los Angeles, I had pared down again—giving away clothes, kitchen items, CDs, videos, books. But still I had what I felt were necessary items basic to my happiness in a foreign country—my grandmother's handstitched quilt, a couple of small Persian rugs, a little Mexican altar, and an oil painting of my tango shoes in an empty suitcase.

I got Phoebe set up with food, water, and a small sand box, while Jorge took a shower in his room next door. After hanging the *No Molestar* sign on the doorknob to keep the maid out and the cat in, we went to Bellas Artes and saw a Frida Kahlo exhibit before lunching at Los Girasoles nearby, my last chance for Mexican food.

To celebrate my final night in Mexico, we went to see my favorite ballet, Swan Lake, performed in Chapultepec Park, danced on islands in a real lake with real swimming swans and boats too. The pageantry with horses and a castle and flaming torches, plus excellent dancing under ancient trees was astounding.

Afterwards we went to Garibaldi Square where the mariachis hang out looking for work three songs at a time. The famous plaza, in a bad part of town, was bustling with many different mariachi groups, all in distinctive regalia. Tourists went there as we did for the ambiance and the music, but that's also where party hosts go to hire a group for a fiesta or a wedding. And in between the colorful groups competing with each other were taco stands and trinket sellers, and of course, beer for sale in paper cups.

Walking back to the hotel along a dark side street, two tall thin young men in tennis shoes ran silently up behind us and demanded our valuables. They took Jorge's money, watch, cell phone, and worst of all, his car keys. Me they frisked, putting their hands in all my pockets, but not finding the purse I carried under my coat. No weapons, no violence, but it was a trauma. I was annoyed at Jorge, who I thought should have known better. I was just following him blindly as he was the Mexican who knew how things were and where not to take the gringa at midnight.

All of my baggage but Phoebe and my carryon were in the van in the hotel. Jorge spent the night with a locksmith down in the garage, who made new keys to the van that contained everything (almost) that I now owned. Phoebe was hidden safely in my room.

Early the next morning at the airport, Jorge helped me with the suitcases and boxes, plus Phoebe and my carryons. For some reason my debit card wouldn't go through at the check-in desk to cover the $350 U.S. excess baggage fees, and the agent tried twice more before sending me to an ATM where it was rejected twice again. I had just used it in the restaurant the day before, and I remembered that on another trip to D.F., after a restaurant charge my American bank had blocked it, assuming the card had been stolen. Luckily I had enough U.S. dollars in cash to pay the baggage charges.

Every bag and box had to be hand-inspected. There were several male security officers on duty, but I had to wait until there was a woman officer available to open everything of mine for inspection. In conservative Mexico, it was inappropriate or maybe even illegal for a man to go through the effects of a woman in case he might touch her packed underwear. But the men were more practiced and faster; I didn't care who touched my "unmentionables", I just wanted to make my flight. I had my bags so tightly crammed it was like a jigsaw puzzle, and the woman just couldn't make everything fit in again. I wasn't allowed to help or touch. So after my careful work, things were stuffed back in willy-nilly and hurriedly sealed with masking tape.

Jorge saw me and Phoebe to the first x-ray security line and we said goodbye, *hasta la vista babies.* I had hired him to bring me to the airport, but over the years we had become good friends and I would miss him. He had helped me a lot during my stay in Mexico. Now he felt embarrassed and ashamed about the mugging, and that I had paid for the locksmith, the hotel, gas, and bought him a new cheap watch.

After Jorge left us, at the x-ray machine the attendant demanded some kind of special paper for Phoebe I had to get at the other end of the airport. I could hardly carry the cat, my two coats, computer, and bag any further, and the plane was due to leave in 30 minutes. But I found a skycap, and he found the Sanitation office, where they fiddled around with all the papers from the vet, making copies, and complaining, and they had to actually look at Phoebe even though she had just been examined by a vet a couple of days previously and given papers of good health. The skycap got me back to the x-ray point, where I took her out of the carrier again, and off we went to the gate. Carrying everything, I thought I would pass out. When we got there the gate had been changed to the other end of the concourse. I almost gave up, but then one of those electric carts came along, and I flagged it down, and the nice man took us almost to the gate. Phoebe can charm anyone.

As I passed the last Duty Free shop, I checked my watch and decided to spend the $10 U.S. I found in my pocket that I didn't know I had. I bought a bracelet and the clerk handed me back my passport and receipt, chatting with the cat. Because I was so near the gate, I clutched my passport in my hand with my ticket and boarding pass. I found the boarding line but when I arrived at the gate, my passport had vanished. I had dropped it, I thought, but more likely someone had plucked it out of my hand. I retraced my steps back to Duty Free, I had three announcements made over the PA system. I asked the custodial people, I all but crawled the entire terminal on my hands and knees, checking every trash can. I couldn't get on the flight without documents. I couldn't enter another country—in this case, Peru, where I was scheduled to change planes for Buenos Aires—without a passport.

I found a pay phone and somehow reached the U.S. Embassy. It was Saturday and no one could help me until Monday.

My six pieces of luggage were unloaded from the plane. I dumped everything out of my carry-on twice in front of the gate staff. I sat down on the floor and sobbed. At last the flight left. I was stupefied. Without Jorge, how could I handle all of that luggage? I couldn't understand anymore all the instructions in Spanish I was receiving. My brain just shut down. I didn't know what to do or how to do it.

I was afraid to leave the airport alone—especially after the mugging. I couldn't deal with having no passport, no money, lots of luggage and a cat, knowing no one in D.F. My friends in San Miguel were four hours away. Finally I cried out,

Por favor, ayudame! And a Taca Airlines person did. He walked me to baggage claim and got two porters to help me through security and explained there were lockers where I could leave my luggage. I had only $4 U.S. for a tip, no Mexican pesos at all. After leaving my boxes (I didn't care what it cost to ransom them out later), I struggled with my big suitcase and carryon and coat along with the cat carrier to find the fancy hotel I had heard was somewhere in the huge airport.

A Mexican man noticed my distress in the concourse and offered in English to help me with my bags. But instead of helping me to the fancy hotel, he made a left turn into a little car rental office, insisting the airport hotel was too expensive and I should stay close to the U.S. Embassy in the Hotel Madrid for one-third the cost.

"But I have no money for a taxi," I explained.

"Don't worry. I'll go with you, the hotel will pay the taxi," he promised.

To get into a taxi with a strange man in Mexico City where it's too dangerous to even hail a cab in the street was not a good idea. Wary and afraid, I snatched my bags and Phoebe and set off for the costly Camino Real Hotel.

Surely they could help me with how to report a missing passport. I knew it was stolen and on its way to Peru, otherwise it would have been immediately found and turned in. I wonder what U.S. passports go for? I was more worried about the debit card that hadn't worked in the airport. I had no cash but Argentinian, but I did have a $1,000 travellers' cheque, which of course required a passport to cash.

I found the hotel office and a willing bellboy to whom I explained I couldn't tip. I must have appeared a wild woman.

I held my breath and the cat carrier under my coat at reception and my debit card got me in because they only took an imprint and didn't run it. I suddenly was in the lap of luxury where I could sign for whatever I needed. Well I needed a drink, so I raided the room's minibar, not caring that the miniscule bottle of vodka and package of pistachios cost almost $15 U.S. I stretched out next to Phoebe on the bed as big as my San Miguel apartment and thanked God.

So I did nothing but order room service and watch pay per view movies with short expensive trips downstairs to the internet. I found a cardboard lid and filled it with popcorn for a sandbox, and fed Phoebe vienna sausages.

I tried calling my bank's 800 number in the States to find out what the problem was with my card, but with or without the operator, I couldn't make the call from the hotel. I called my friend Holly in Los Angeles collect, and she called the bank on her other line while I held on, and got the problem straightened out. The bank had blocked the card when it was put through twice at check-in and then twice more when I tried to get cash at the ATM. They had assumed it was stolen.

Monday morning I used the hotel's ATM while crossing my fingers, and cash came out! Mexican pesos in hand I took a $25 U.S. ride to the U.S. Embassy, had my picture taken and within an hour had my temporary U.S. Passport, which I kissed lovingly—the ticket to freedom (along with money). They were happy to accept a personal check. I now understood the joy of seeing the American flag in a foreign country.

During the next day I ran around the airport getting my unused ticket and Phoebe's to Buenos Aires exchanged for

Wednesday. To keep the maid out, I left the Do Not Disturb sign always on the door.

I hated to leave the womb of the hotel on Wednesday and dive into the mess of the Mexico City airport, the worse I've ever done time in. I paid the ransom for my boxes, lavishly tipped anyone who helped me, and thanked God my debit card got me out of that hotel. At least during my four days of incarceration, I was comfortable, well fed, and rested. Maybe it was meant to happen.

I replayed the scene from Saturday: checking in, security underwear check, inspection of Phoebe, and got to the gate with plenty of time to spare. No shopping at the Duty Free.

Then at the door of the plane, they wouldn't let me take Phoebe without the captain's OK. I waved the ticket in their faces and said, "Well then, get the Captain out here!" I explained to him the agony of the preceding days, showed him the tickets, and reminded him that during the summer months it was against international laws for live animals to be transported in the baggage hold. He begrudgingly let us enter; I think he saw I was at my breaking point.

Once on board, in the back of a full flight with Phoebe at my feet, I started to relax, when the attendant said the cat couldn't fly in the cabin but had to go with the luggage. I demanded to talk to the captain, I argued with every attendant, I raced back and forth and up and down the aisle. Everyone told me something different: people complained, people were allergic, there was no space. Finally they simply ripped the carrier out of my hands. In the meantime I was crying hysterically, and the people around me agreed to change around their seats to make more room, and I ran to tell the attendant. But it made no difference. I had been assured when I bought my ticket she could ride in the cabin as it was too hot in BsAs for her to survive the landing at this time of year. I paid $300 more to fly on Taca just because of Phoebe. During the entire nine-hour flight I thought that surely she wouldn't make it. I was heart sick. But she survived.

The only luggage of my six pieces that arrived with me was my painting. I never had any fun I didn't pay for, one way or another.

CHAPTER 37

MIDNIGHT SERVICE
AT THE CHURCH OF TANGO

*Tango querido, siento que tiemblan las baldosas
de un bailongo y oigo el rezongo de mi pasado...*

~ Enrique Santos Discépolo, writer of tangos

Back in Buenos Aires for the umpteenth time in seven years, this time it was permanent. My tango articles were successful in many print magazines such as *Skirt!* and *Dancing Times*, and I needed more material, but I also needed to dance. I had preferred to dance flamenco in Mexico and to wait for the chance to visit Argentina to dance tango, but now I had made the big move across the Equator, and I was in Buenos Aires with Phoebe and my remaining worldly goods.

Until I could find an apartment to rent, I once again stayed with Cristina Lopez in the middle-class neighborhood of Caballito, who didn't mind that I had Phoebe, by now a seasoned traveler used to staying in just one room. Three other rooms in the apartment were filled with dancers from Sweden, Germany, and Canada, and of course Cristina was a tanguera too. Whenever any of us met up with each other in the kitchen or the lone bathroom, we had plenty to talk about. Every day we all discussed who danced where and with whom and how, because tango was all that mattered.

One Friday night Cristina drove me and her other house guests to Sin Rumbo. The historic club was far out of town, but famous as the "birthplace of tango." Cristina called it the real "church of tango," the genuine tango cathedral. Utterly different from the smoky and dark La Catédral that was the underground funky club of the moment, at Sin Rumbo the harsh overhead fluorescent lighting illuminated a dozen people seated at tables and a few couples on the small, black and white checkered tile floor. One couple caught my eye: a middle-aged pair a foot apart performing complicated figures with bored faces. "Married too long," observed Cristina. I was reminded of the couple I saw dancing long ago in the Casino d'Evian in France, who had no tango skills, but a strong connection, just the opposite of these people who skillfully and passionlessly were now maneuvering the floor.

Torquato Tasso was another modest, cramped, inelegant old tango hall, yet famous nevertheless. I wanted to leave by two a.m., as it was crowded, smoky and hot. But when twelve white-haired portly men in tuxedos took the small stage, I hung around. A U.S. fire inspector would have kicked out the people clogging the staircase, blocking the doorways. It was hotter than Carnival in Cuba. You couldn't squeeze between the tables to go to the bathroom, and yet people danced.

As I stared at the five bandoneonistas holding the heavy instruments on their laps lovingly like girlfriends, I asked Cristina, "Do you agree that the bandoneon is the sexiest instrument a man can play?"

"Ooh yes!" she laughed. "Just look how they hold it!"

It was an observation, not of the particular musicians, but of tango—tango performed with skill and passion. And just then, one of the bandoneon players leaned forward, almost resting his cheek on the bellows, as if he were caressing his lover.

Still, just as I loved the politesse of the French people, I loved being treated like a woman in Argentina, the only place in the world where I was happy to be called a "girl," (*chica*—in the milongas, all the women are chicas even if they are eighty years old; the men are *muchachos*.) I loved the men who danced with a handkerchief in their hand so as not to get yours sweaty, the men who gave you poems, who held you firmly and with assurance, the men who told you how beautiful you were, how well you danced in a way that made you almost believe it, the men who apologized for coming to your table but who were desperate to dance with you and you wouldn't look at them, the tango shoe salesman who prostrated himself on the floor and kissed your feet tired from hours of dancing, the men passing you on the street who said, not, "Hey, baby, want to get a beer?", but "For a kiss from your lips I will give you my heart." Who didn't enjoy seeing the old man who could hardly walk hobble to meet his partner on the floor and lead her with technique and perfect rhythm in a dance she enjoyed?

After twelve years of loneliness and searching, of trying so hard to live and be happy, I felt satisfied in the milongas of Buenos Aires. I danced all night and wrote by day. For me, the physical and spiritual utterly connected and intertwined in such a life. I had always preferred a pas de deux to a solo. And the thousands of ordinary people like me in Buenos Aires, who congregated every day to dance with no compromises or outside expectations, all valued the same thing—the dance. For the same reasons that people enjoyed the group experience of theater and concerts, that comedies were funnier and tragedies more devastating when shared, I was at peace dancing along with the hundreds of like-minded people in a tango salon.

I longed terribly for my children but had to be content with occasional visits, email, and phone calls—way too few as far as I was concerned. But young men had their lives to lead, whether their mother was in the same city or country or not. I still ached for Jack and always would. Living in a small rental apartment in a working class barrio in Buenos Aires was nothing like my life had been in Los Angeles. If I had kept my beautiful house, sacrificing everything to make the payments and maintenance, it would have been free and clear now, with the mortgage paid off. But I would have missed the dance.

I had never been to La Confiteria Ideal at night, but when La Orquesta de los Reyes de Tango performed, I showed up at midnight in January for the one a.m. concert. Summer in the old salon without air conditioning meant the hall was hot and humid with the crowds dancing and perspiring under the dark Art Nouveau skylight, the big wall fans swirling the women's skirts as they turned about the marble floor. Waiters carried stacks of chairs overhead to the salon's far corners as more people crowded in. The ladies' beating Spanish fans kept time to the music and were all that moved outside the dance floor, the focus of everyone's attention. The mirrors on the wood-paneled walls reflected young hip dancers of Tango Nuevo, old milongueros, local porteños, and international tourists of all ages in the dim light of old globe chandeliers and sconces.

We all had a single purpose, to hear these elderly men, the Kings of Tango, play just as they had in their heyday of the forties and fifties. The couples on the floor moved to the music as one, slowing together, speeding up in concert with the orchestra, creating their own special accompaniment—the swish-hush-glide of bodies in motion, fabric rustles, leather soles caressing the floor. It felt choreographed, that we all were enclosed in one embrace. The hot floor was a pheromone furnace. The watchers as well as the dancers were soaked with sweat from their hair through their clothes, but it felt clean and natural.

I wished Cristina had been there, Marisol, Nancy, Holly, Adam and Jason, Jack, my mother, my dad, Edith and Floriane and Mémé from Lugrin, Olivier, I wished everyone I had ever loved had been there. It was a delightful orgy, a celebration, of heat, sweat and passionate connection of all kinds of people to each other, the music, and the cosmos. It was Heaven.

CHAPTER 38

TANGO IN THE CATHEDRAL

Se abrio el cielo y bajaron los angeles?
Heavens opened and the angels came down?

~ Piropo (compliment) heard on the street in Buenos Aires

It was known as La Catédral. Not easy to find in Buenos Aires' dark side streets at three in the morning--no signs, no cars, no people hanging around in front smoking. From the second floor of the old wooden warehouse came the siren call of tango music. It was eerie and scary, mounting those stairs alone, but I was helpless to do otherwise, a pilgrim drawn to the altar of Tango.

The room was huge, like the inside of a barn, all wood. It was barely lit by large candelabra with most of the candles melted into pools of silky wax, some votive flames, and a few strings of fairy lights. It smelled of cat piss and dusky marijuana. A bar ran the width of the room in back, with enormous, bright modern paintings hanging all the way to the rafters. Shadowy figures were sitting around the room on the lumpy funky old couches and broken chairs, their conversations punctuated by the smoldering ends of their cigarettes moving in the dark. At first I could only see the silhouettes of dancers through the smoke. Three or four couples on the warped, uneven wooden dance floor, moved, not to traditional Pugliese or Tanturi, but to Louis Armstrong's "Kiss of Fire."

Someone approached out of the gloom. *Quieres bailar?* He was young, muscular, handsome, with black-rimmed glasses framing eyes that sparkled with chemical excitement. He was so tall I had to reach up very high to wrap my left arm around his neck. He held me tight and led me with brute machismo, so unlike the subtle leads of the old milongueros I had danced with at Club Almagro earlier that night. When I leaned against him in the traditional tango pose of female trust, he dragged me across the floor, lifted me back on my feet, turned and twisted me, giving me no opportunity to embellish or decorate his steps. I simply obeyed. It was different, exhilarating, exhausting.

"You don't really need to work out at the gym, do you?" I panted during a break in the music.

"No, I eat red Argentine beef full of blood! Blood! To make me strong!" His eyes glittered, muscles rippled under his tight tee shirt, testosterone energy creating an almost visible aura around him.

Breathless, I had to sit out the next set and recover on an old velvet sofa next to a dozing cat. I watched people arriving and leaving in the candlelight, with their high-heeled tango shoes, jeans, and backpacks. The informality of the setting and the dancers' attire and attitude clashed with the ceremonial tango they danced so seriously.

After years of running from illness, loneliness and loss, I at last knew where to find peace. Sitting at a table drinking *sidra* with friends, sometimes going to tango heaven with a remarkable dancer, stepping—sweaty and spent—into a waiting taxi at five a.m. and driving home through the quiet dawn; climbing into bed with that sweet body and soul exhaustion that connects me to the universe—I didn't want more than that. Upon discovering tango, many people dream of finding an honest and kind, monogamous, good-looking, superb dance partner who was single and looking for a relationship. The tango experience--profound, sensuous and spiritual--made us confuse the dancer with the dance. Whether a man was young or old, handsome or not, single or married—all that mattered to me now was the brief glimpse of the Universe that we saw together on the dance floor.

Tango was invitation, wanting, rejection, needing, spiritual connection, sensuality, attitude, sex—the themes of my life during the past decade of suffering and knowledge. On my first Buenos Aires trip many years ago in 1997, every time I was asked to dance I got palpitations and couldn't breathe. I wore opaque dark tights and shapeless dresses and English ballroom shoes I found in the back of my closet. When I first wore a short skirt, a really short skirt, to dance in Los Angeles, my legs in sheer black stockings and high heels shook so badly I could hardly walk up the stairs. When I didn't die or shock anyone to death, tight and short dresses became my tango uniform. As my tango became proficient, I became proud of my body, even at my age.

Now here in Buenos Aires, Carlos Gavito, Omar Vega, and other tango superstars approached me as if they were just anybody--or I was someone. At Club Gricel, I was afraid to look at Gavito for fear that he would think me too aggressive.

I had taken a few lessons from him in Los Angeles when he was on tour with "Forever Tango," so we knew each other a little. At the milongas, Gavito only danced with the best and the youngest women. Yet, from the corner of my eye, I saw him stand up, button his jacket, and walk around the dance floor to my table. I glanced behind me for the woman who was the object of his invitation, but I was the one who held his eyes. When he returned me to my table ten minutes later, the local women sitting with me were astonished. I could just hear the whispers: "Who is *she*?"

One afternoon in Buenos Aires, I danced an impromptu demonstration in Parque Rivadavia with Ernesto, a handsome milonguero who owned only the elegant suit of clothes on his back. We tangoed to music from a boombox tied to the bicycle of a grizzled old man beneath the arching branches of a huge fig tree. Elderly couples, young children, a woman in a wheelchair, drew round cheering, and threw money and candy at us while we danced under the high green canopy of leaves. What a blessing to be dancing in this "chapel" of fellow believers. It was a miracle that I could glide so gracefully over the rough bricks in backless high wedgies with rubber soles. It was a miracle that my twelve years of journeying towards the light put me just here, just now. Maybe I made mistakes, maybe I've had to pay for them, maybe I've had bad luck and loss, maybe I'm not young and am alone, maybe my loved ones are gone, but I am here and dancing, dancing, dancing, blessed and happy.

Thank God I had prayed at La Catédral!

AFTERWORD

UNA TANDA MÁS

Let us dance this tango, I do not want to yearn.
Tomorrow, my ship will sail away.

~ from "Mañana zarpa un barco"
a tango by Jorge I. Oclander

I hate to leave a milonga. I say to my friend or myself, *Una tanda más*. Let's not go yet--let's see what the next set brings. I don't want to leave the place where I feel most at home. I don't want to leave the place where I know what the rules are, where I feel in control, where my skills are recognized and appreciated. In my heart I am always waiting to dance La Cumparsita, the traditional final tango, but I'm not in a hurry. I want to postpone it as long as possible. The tables of men who look like a casting call for The Godfather, the rows of sultry women smoking cigarettes with crossed legs, the man who rhapsodizes on the reasons I am so elegant when I dance, the endless discussions of the music and orchestras, the men who "love" me and press their phone numbers into my hand, the teacher who tries every trick in his repertoire in order to make his partner want lessons with him, the elegant Maitre'ds who remember where I like to sit, the men who show off their fanciest steps in front of the tables of their friends, the waiters and waitresses who tirelessly kiss me hello and goodbye while serving me until dawn in the smoky salons, the women in the bathrooms who sell sexy tango clothes, the taxi drivers who sing tangos on the way to the milonga, the collective intake of breath with the first notes of Pavadita or the Pugliese tanda—this was my world now.

And I hope there will always be *una tanda más* for you and for me.

13954719R00175

Made in the USA
Lexington, KY
29 February 2012